LEAH CRUMP

Be Well, Do Well

A Field Guide to Work That Heals, Leadership That Lasts, and Living Well on Your Own Terms

First published by Leah Crump Consulting 2025

Copyright © 2025 by Leah Crump

All rights reserved. No part of this publication may be reproduced, stored or transmitted in any form or by any means, electronic, mechanical, photocopying, recording, scanning, or otherwise without written permission from the publisher. It is illegal to copy this book, post it to a website, or distribute it by any other means without permission.

For permissions, media inquiries, or licensing opportunities, visit: www.leahcrump.com

First edition

Illustration by Yasira Crump
Cover art by Kate Sullivan

This book was professionally typeset on Reedsy. Find out more at reedsy.com

Contents

Be Well, Do Well	iv
Dedication	v
A Definition of Wellness	vi
Forward	vii
An Introduction	xi
A Warm Invitation	xv
1 Fairy Town	1
2 Initiated by Care	16
3 Running With Wolves	53
4 The Business of Being Well	72
5 When the Body Speaks	88
6 The Repatterning	101
7 Arrival and Still Waters	129
8 Living Well on My Own Terms	154
Dearest Reader	161
A Remembering	162
A Final Blessing	164
Acknowledgments	165
Your Turn	168
If This Book Met You at the Right Time...	169
Field Guide Index	170

Be Well, Do Well

A Field Guide to Work That Heals, Leadership That Lasts,
and Living Well on Your Own Terms

~

From The Voice of a New Era in Wellness and Leadership
Leah Crump

Dedication

For my family—Kaya, Yasira, and Atreju
You are the heart of everything that matters.

Kaya, thank you for walking with me through every season, for holding the line when I couldn't, and for loving me in all forms. Yasira, your brilliance, humor, and grounded intuition keep me both inspired and honest. Atreju, your calm wisdom and quiet fire remind me what it means to live with presence.

This book was shaped in the spaces between us. It carries our love, our resilience, and a truth I now live by: wellness and leadership can rise together.

A Definition of Wellness

Definition of Well, adj.

1. Aligned in body, spirit, and strategy.
2. Resourced enough to rest.
3. Unbothered by perfection.
4. In possession of one's own rhythm.
5. Willing to live fully, even when things are messy.

"Being well isn't about resolution. It's about returning, again and again." - Leah Crump

Forward

A Note from Behind the Pages: The Making of this Book
This book is divided around three interconnected themes: work that heals, leadership that lasts, and living well on your own terms. You'll see these reflected not in theory, but in lived experience. I've created space in these pages for you to track how these principles show up in your own story. What's healing, what's lasting, and what's finally yours.

There were days I felt completely clear, and others where I sat in front of the page with nothing but the ache of wanting it to be good.

I didn't write this book because I had it all figured out. I wrote it because I finally stopped trying to. And in that surrender, something deeper came forward. Not the voice of the consultant or the achiever or the perfectionist, but the voice of the woman who's lived this life. Who has learned to pause and breathe and try to ask better questions.

Who knows that softness is strength. That clarity can change everything. And stories... especially the honest, imperfect ones... have power.

If you feel any part of yourself in these pages, that's not a coincidence. It means we're walking on similar terrain. It means some piece of my story sparks something in yours. And for me, that is the deepest privilege of all.

This book came out of years of listening to clients, to colleagues, to women at every stage of life and leadership. But more than anything, it came from listening to the quiet voice within. The one I ignored for years. The one that kept whispering: tell the truth, hold the vision, trust the timing.

So I finally did.

Sometimes that meant getting up early to write while the house was still. Other times it meant voice-noting chapters from the passenger seat on a road trip, or walking through memories I hadn't revisited in a decade. It meant asking myself hard questions, opening old wounds, and remembering that I've always been more than "just" a wellness professional. I've always been a seeker. A storyteller. A woman who believes in the sacred rhythm of personal evolution.

And to be honest, I almost didn't finish. Not because I didn't want to, but because I wasn't sure if the world would receive one more voice in a vast sea of content. But then I remembered: we don't write to be the loudest, we write to tell our truth.

So if this book found its way to you, I trust it's because something in your spirit was ready for it.

I was ready to remember that beauty isn't performance, it's presence. That success is not a title, it's alignment. That wellness is not an aesthetic, it's a reclamation.

And that the future is not something to fear, but something we create.

You don't have to be perfect to build a life you love. You just have to be honest, curious, and willing to begin again. That's what I did on every page here... I returned again and again. And I'm so deeply grateful you're coming with me.

So thank you, dear reader, for reading, for witnessing, and for carrying this forward into your own work, in your own way, through your own story.

There's more ahead for us all. I can feel it.

With love,
 -*Leah*

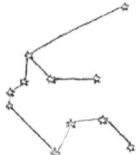

An Introduction

Have you ever stood at the threshold of something new, like a career path, a personal project, or a fresh perspective, and felt both excited and terrified at the same time? If so, you're in the right place. Maybe you've wondered whether it's truly possible to build a life that honors your deepest values while pursuing your loftiest goals. Perhaps you've felt a spark in your chest that whispers, "There's more out there for me", but you're not entirely sure how to blend that sense of calling with your real-world responsibilities and constraints.

I've been there. In fact, I've sat down to write this book countless times, across many years, each time pausing to question: How can I share my journey in a way that both resonates with others and remains true to who I am? I'm not here to claim I have all the answers. It's really quite the contrary. I'm here to share the stories, hard-earned lessons, and flashes of insight that have shaped me into someone who believes, wholeheartedly, that we can *be well* while we *do well*.

I learned this lesson not from a single, dramatic epiphany but from a series of everyday moments: my earliest memories in my grandfather's greenhouse in Portland, Oregon, a childhood themed around the ache of exclusion and loneliness, the enthralling discovery of the healing arts, a decades-long love story that stood up to racism, and an ongoing commitment to blending wellness with entrepreneurship. Each step of my path has helped me understand what it means to live authentically, build meaningful connections, and keep growing, even in the face of failure or heartbreak.

If you've ever asked yourself: "Can I truly create a life that feels as good on the inside as it may look on the outside? I want to assure you that the answer is yes. It doesn't come from forcing yourself into a rigid set of rules, nor does it appear overnight like magic. It emerges gradually, like seedlings in a well-tended greenhouse—developing roots, stretching toward the light, and flourishing under consistent care and pruning.

This book is meant to be a field guide, not a foolproof manual. In these pages, I weave together personal stories, reflections, and lessons gleaned from years of working at the intersection of wellness and business. My goal is to spark something in you. An idea, a conviction, or perhaps a quiet reassurance that you're not alone in this pursuit. In truth, many of us long to do well in a way that doesn't drain our essence.

So I invite you to come along. Bring your wonderings, your hopes, your lingering doubts. Let's explore how to create spaces of belonging, how to navigate life's transitions, how to cultivate meaningful relationships, and how to hold onto our sense of wholeness while moving purposefully toward success. My hope is that you'll feel empowered, energized, and, above all, *reminded* that you already have what it takes to live out your vision, from a place of profound well-being.

Your Journey, Entwined with Mine

Looking back at the winding path that led me here, and the stories I'll tell you, through our family greenhouse in Portland, Oregon, complexities of a blended family, wonder of discovering the healing arts, the challenge of balancing wellness and business, the fierce drive to ensure no one feels excluded, and the enduring love that frames my world—I can see that every stage was necessary. Each step taught me something about compassion, resilience, and the power of meaningful relationships.

Now, I want to encourage *you*: as you turn the page on this Introduction and step into the next part of the book, be open to your own transformation. Perhaps you'll be reminded of long-forgotten dreams. Maybe you'll see new possibilities in your current circumstances. Or you might realize you have a strong "why" for building something remarkable, and all you need are a few supportive insights to help you do it.

No matter what your story looks like so far, remember this: you already carry the seeds of belonging, growth, and purpose within you. I offer you sunlight, water, and some gentle tending, so that those seeds can flourish into something far beyond your expectations.

A Warm Invitation

I invite you to step into the stories that shaped me, and I invite you to reflect on your own.

Have you ever felt an unspoken longing for a deeper kind of success—one that nourishes your spirit as much as it fills your bank account? Have you ever sensed that your relationships, both personal and professional, could be more fulfilling if only you had the time or courage to invest in them fully? Have you ever known, deep down, that you deserve a life where wellness and purpose walk hand in hand?

If you have, let's walk together. Through these pages, I'll share the compass I used to live well while doing well. You'll find practical strategies, guided reflections, and imperfect, real-life ruminations designed to help you integrate these insights into your own journey. We'll play with themes like authenticity, love, resilience, redefining success, forging meaningful connections, owning your power through choice, and living your purpose every day.

Think of these chapters as stepping stones, each one building on the last to help you craft a life that honors who you are at your core. As a creative and positive-mindset thinker, I'm here to remind you that there's no one-size-fits-all formula. Instead, there is a tapestry of experiences, tools, and perspectives that you can weave into your unique story.

Perhaps the greatest lesson I've learned along the way is that we can't do this alone. Just as seeds need soil, sun, water, and the occasional tending hand, we humans flourish when we're cared for and when we care for others in return. Whether it's family, friends, mentors, or even the supportive voice of a well-timed book, the right kind of guidance can make all the difference between stagnation and growth.

The Lessons That Anchor This Book
My story is a testament to a few core themes that I believe can guide anyone seeking to build a life of authentic living and purposeful business:

1. Belonging Is a Prerequisite for Growth
Whether it's the greenhouse in my grandfather's backyard, a blended family dinner table, or a supportive circle of friends, the spaces we create for each other shape our capacity to dream and evolve.

2. Transitions Can Be a Spark for Transformation
Moves, new family dynamics, new ventures, shifting roles in life—every transition can carry both anxiety and possibility. Leaning into the latter can unlock strengths you never knew you had.

3. Nurturing Yourself Is Part of the Equation
Wellness isn't a reward to be claimed after you've worked yourself to the bone. It's the bedrock that sustains real, lasting success.

4. Balance Grows Where Perfectionism Ends
By abandoning the quest for flawlessness, you give yourself room to breathe, iterate, and find true alignment with your values.

5. Enduring Love Is a Choice
Real love, whether romantic, familial, or communal, requires daily acts of presence, kindness, and steadfast commitment.

So are you ready? Let's begin.

1

Fairy Town

Before I had the language for it, I was already chasing a life that let me be well and do well. I didn't want to choose between purpose and peace. I still don't.

"We are shaped by what we remember – and what we never stop believing is real."

Some childhoods are marked by wounds, others by wonder. Mine had both. I didn't grow up in a picture-perfect world, but I grew up in a world full of feeling. One of beauty, longing, and of curiosity about what makes people feel seen and whole. There was grief and loss, yes, but also magic. Whispers in the wind. Sacred pauses between the noise. A sense that something else was at work, something gentle and protective. I didn't have the language for it back then, but I would later come to understand that those early moments weren't just memories. They were messages.

As a child, I made tea from bits of plants and flowers I found in the garden. Not to drink it, but simply for the joy of making it. I'd stir it with reverence of an old-world healer. I'd speak to the bees. Our barn had a natural hive, and they never once stung me. I'd walk barefoot near them, talking softly, as if I were part of their world. Maybe I was.

That invisible world, what I later came to think of as Fairy Town, wasn't about fantasy. It was about feeling connected. To the land, to something spiritual, to something eternal. It felt like the edge of a veil that hadn't closed yet.

What if your sensitivity wasn't a flaw, but a finely

tuned compass? What if every strange, beautiful moment you sensed in your childhood was quietly preparing you to be who you are now?

The scent of my grandfather's garden. The rhythm of family gatherings. The quiet ache of being on the outside looking in. All of it would shape not just who I became, but how I would build a life rooted in presence, beauty, and wellness.

Wellness is about belonging. It's about healing the places where we once felt lost. It's about remembering what it feels like to be cared for... really cared for... when the world outside is chaotic.

But before I could offer that to others, I had to understand where it came from.

A Childhood Rooted in Beauty and Connection
I grew up in Portland, Oregon, surrounded by trees so tall they felt like ancient protectors. Our home was tucked inside what felt like its own little dimension, a secret world layered with green. There was moss on the steps, ivy along the fence, and a thick stillness in the air after the rain that made everything feel alive.

My mom, an artist with a free spirit, created a home

that didn't always make sense, but always made magic. She painted. She sculpted. She found color in things most people overlooked. She saw the world through color and shape and symbolism. Her way of understanding me was visual. She could see beauty I couldn't yet articulate. But she wasn't the strong, unshakable archetype we often glorify. She was soft, and had her own shadows, much of which I still don't know the details of. Today I understand it as emotional unavailability. Back then, I was simply on my own.

My mom was a truly single mother. She'd never married or had a real connection with my birth father. We lived within a close-knit circle that included my grandparents, my aunt, my uncle, and my cousin. Looking back, I see how these early experiences showed me that a family doesn't have to fit a strict formula to offer love and belonging. Still, the absence of a traditional father figure hung in the air, a reminder that something was missing.

Our old house had a wraparound porch, a sunroom where the light danced through lace curtains, and a stone fire oven in the back that smelled of smoke and rosemary. The yard overflowed with life. We had rows of berries. Blackberries, strawberries, raspberries, and they stained our fingers by mid-summer. There was corn, there were fruit trees, there were herbs tucked into corners like secrets: basil, mint, rosemary, lavender. And there was a wooden arbor covered in grapevines, shading the patio where people always gathered.

We lived with my grandparents, and the family home was a world within a world to me. My grandpa was a man of the earth. A gardener, yes, but also a Freemason, and philosopher of soil and silence. I was his shadow, trailing behind him through his orchard, greenhouse, and berry patches like it was church. He taught me how to tend and how to listen. How to smell the difference between over watered soil and healthy growth. He'd kneel beside me, showing me how to place seeds in neat rows, how to water them just enough, offering a subtle lesson in consistency and stewardship. These moments planted in me the idea that nurturing is a way of life—one that would later become the cornerstone of my approach to wellness.

I remember always having the food I needed, warmth and care. But I also felt like I was subtly being encouraged to become self-sufficient. I intuitively watched the emotional tides of my household closely. I learned how to read the room before I entered it, and knew how visible I should be.

And while I never felt unsafe, far from it, I did feel cherished and well loved, and also felt the unspoken pressure of making my own way.

The greenhouse was my sanctuary. It smelled like earth and light, like something eternal. Walking through a nursery still takes me back there. That scent, the mixture of damp soil and tender green, reminds me who I am.

I remember my grandma's rose garden, too, where a little stone donkey stood watch in the center. I'd sit on that statue while she pruned and clipped, gently asking the roses what they needed. I didn't know it then, but those small, ordinary moments would one day become the architecture of my entire belief system: that beauty heals. That the simplest forms of care—gardening, gathering, touch, attention, are sometimes the most sacred.

If you've ever felt gratitude for the life you've been given mingled with a longing for what's absent, you understand the complexity of my early childhood. It was equal parts magical and bittersweet, a "Fairy Town" where I learned that small acts of care could transform the everyday into something extraordinary, even if some forms of support or guidance were missing.

You don't have to be mystical to relate. Maybe your knowing came through dreams, or journaling, or just a gut feeling you were meant for more. However it arrived, you weren't imagining it.

The Potlucks That Built Me
Family potlucks were my first taste of community. Of belonging. Not the polished kind, but the messy, wonderful kind, with kids running through sprinklers, cousins piling food onto paper plates, someone always forgetting the forks. We gathered often. My family, our extended kin, friends, neighbors, people who just happened to show up and stay. My memory of those potlucks is layered: the smell of grilled corn, the sound of folding chairs scraping against the patio bricks, the ripple of conversation that moved like music.

Those were the moments where I felt a kind of rightness. No roles to perform, no achievements required. Just food, presence, laughter, and being together. They shaped my understanding of community and hospitality, not the curated kind, but the real kind. The kind where you bring what you have, and it's enough.

Even one memory of true belonging can become a blueprint. What moments in your life showed you what a community could feel like, before the world taught you to settle for less?

Weird Dreams and Astral Travels
Even though we were surrounded by relatives and the constant hum of visitors, I often played independently. I'm sure someone was always nearby. Grandma Doris outside hanging linens, Mom in the kitchen making lunch, but I remember feeling quietly alone in the most comforting way. Not exactly lonely. Not unsupervised. Just... free.

Certain places on the property carried a protective energy: the old stairwell, the sunroom upstairs, the long rows of berry bushes, the patch of hydrangeas along the southern fence line. Smokey the cat and Chico the little rescue dog were usually nearby, adding to the sense that I was being looked after. There was a feeling, otherworldly, not frightening, that I was protected from afar.

It was during these years that my dreams began to change. I started having vivid, intense dreams, images and experiences that didn't feel made up. As I grew older, around nine or ten, those dreams became more structured. Every night, I would fall asleep with a sense of expectation, preparing to visit what I called my special place.

In these dreams, I'd start in the woods, a different entry point each time, and would follow a quiet inner compass to an opening in the earth. On the walk, I was never alone. An animal would always appear. Sometimes a bunny or a frog, but most often, a red fox. The fox was my guide. Together, we'd arrive at a cluster of boulders and a rocky crevice, my portal. We'd enter a dim cavern where I'd pick up a tiny torch. The fox would light it with a flick of magic, casting the softest glow.

We'd walk deeper into the earth, and I always sensed I wasn't alone. The shadows felt alive, full of creatures peering out from the rocks. Large spiders, I always imagined, watching from their quiet corners. But I never turned back. I wasn't afraid, not exactly. I was curious. Connected. On a mission I couldn't quite name.

These travels became part of my rhythm. I didn't talk about them, and they didn't feel strange to me, they just felt true. I wouldn't have called it astral travel then, but I know now that it was a form of exploration. A way of visiting the inner and outer edges of myself. And it would later add a unique layer to my understanding of wellness. Not just physical or emotional, but deeply spiritual and unseen.

What is the place that only you will ever know and understand? Can you think of it now? Can you feel what it was like to be there again? If you can, maybe you can remember too that the person who walked in that space lives in you today.

Learning the Edges of Belonging
My mother raised me on her own for much of my early life. She did the best she could, and her creativity left a permanent imprint on me. But life shifted when someone new came into our world, my adoptive step-dad. I call him my Dad now, because that's who he became to me.

He wasn't loud in his love, but it was steady. He taught me the art of showing up, over and over again. He drove me to practices and tournaments all across the Pacific Northwest, no matter the hour, no matter the distance. He listened when I didn't have the words. And when he couldn't say things out loud, he wrote to me, long, mostly encouraging letters on yellow-lined legal pads. I kept those. I still have some of them.

It's only with time that I've been able to recognize what a gift that kind of consistency was. He didn't try to fix me. He didn't make a show of things. He just showed up.

That kind of presence gets into your bones. It taught me that care doesn't always look like grand gestures, it looks like dependability, like kindness without commentary. That understanding would later shape the way I show up for others, in business, in friendship, in leadership.

Still, being part of a blended family came with its complications. Love was present, but not always evenly distributed. There were unspoken lines I couldn't quite cross. If you've ever felt like an afterthought in a room full of people, you understand how that feeling can seep in.

That feeling shaped me in ways I wouldn't fully understand until later. It made me fiercely inclusive. If you're in my world, you're in. No question. No caveats.

That instinct has followed me through every season of life. Whether it's welcoming a stranger into conversation, making sure someone overlooked in a meeting gets their say, or creating wellness experiences where no one feels left out, I've built my entire professional foundation on one simple belief: we're all going together.

Movement as Medicine

By the time I reached my teenage years, life was a swirl of team sports, awkward growth spurts, and the social gymnastics of high school in the '90s. And while those years brought their own challenges, they also brought me closer to my body, in a good way.

Sports became my anchor. I played on high-level teams, traveled to clinics and camps, and began to understand my body not just as something to manage or control, but as a source of strength. Movement helped me feel powerful in a world that was constantly telling girls to shrink.

This was the era of heroine-chic beauty standards, thin, waifish, borderline invisible. The pressure was real, but I had other messages coming through: from teammates, from the court, from my own endurance. I wasn't just a body to be looked at. I was a body that could do.

And through it all, my Dad was there. Driving, watching, showing up. Sometimes quietly, sometimes with a letter waiting on the kitchen counter when I got home. That kind of support gave me something many girls don't get: a sense of being backed. Not because I was perfect, but because I mattered.

Then, at 15, my baby brother was born.
And everything changed.

He became my person. My heart outside my body. Suddenly, I wasn't just navigating my own life, I was modeling what it meant to live with heart. That shift gave me purpose in a new way. It lit something in me that has never gone out.

Grief, Grounding, and the Quiet Pull of Purpose
Of course, those years weren't without loss. My grandparents, those pillars of beauty and wisdom, passed away. My parents separated. Grief moved into our house like an uninvited guest and refused to leave.

There were moments when I thought I might break. Moments I look back on now and realize how easy it would've been to go down a darker path.

But I didn't.
Because I had anchors.

Real friendships instead of toxic ones. The grounding power of movement and nature. A brother who reminded me that love could be simple and unconditional. And a growing love for beauty and wellness that had been planted in me long ago, now stretching toward the light.

Fairy Town Today
As a child, Fairy Town felt like a place. A secret dimension tucked inside the folds of the Pacific Northwest. But now I see it differently. It wasn't a place. It was a way of being. A state where I felt connected, safe, seen, by the earth, by my ancestors, by something beyond the veil.

This chapter of my life taught me the difference between escape and imagination.

It taught me how to listen without needing proof.

And most of all, it taught me that beauty is not a performance, it's a frequency. Certain places leave imprints in us. What spaces still live in your memory, not because they were grand, but because they made you feel held?

Fairy Town was my blueprint: not for escape, but for return.

Let This Be Your Beginning, Too
Maybe you've been circling your own path, waiting to land. Maybe you've felt the sting of exclusion, or the ache of not quite belonging. Maybe you've

followed instincts that didn't make sense at the time, but they led you somewhere sacred anyway.

This book isn't just about my story. It's about yours, too. Your childhood clues. Your sacred places. You're quiet knowing.

You're not behind. You're right on time.

Return to one memory from childhood where you felt deeply safe or alive. What does that moment reveal about the way you're wired for wellness? What pieces of that version of you might still be guiding your present-day self?

2

Initiated by Care

Enduring Love: The Foundation of a Life Well Lived

"Sometimes your real life begins when you stop trying to understand your origin story."

Pause here for a moment. What's showing up in your body? What part of you wants to be seen right now, not fixed?

When I was five my mother met and soon after married my stepfather, who soon became my adoptive father—and expanded our world significantly. I gained step-siblings, new aunts, uncles, cousins, and a new grandmother - Lillian - who instantly embraced me. In a swirl of family introductions, my life changed almost overnight. Where I once felt the absence of a father, I now had a dad who consistently and steadily showed up every single day.

This dad became extremely important to me, a positive influence who taught me about responsibility, work ethic, and the gentle power of showing up when it matters. He didn't try to replace the father I never had; he simply became the father I did have, offering a kind of stability and acceptance that I didn't realize I'd craved. We had family dinners where everyone was welcome, holiday gatherings that merged extended families into one, and the occasional chaotic hustle of having more siblings under one roof. If you've ever lived through a blended family transition, you'll know it can be both disorienting and deeply enriching.

I learned early on that "belonging" isn't always automatic, even within a loving environment. Sometimes it takes intentional choices—from both sides—to make someone feel seen and valued. My dad wasn't perfect, nor was I, but through small daily interactions (a pat on the back, a ride to sports practice, a genuine interest in my day), he communicated, You are wanted here.

My Dad wrote me over 100 letters of encouragement and lessons throughout my young life on his yellow legal pad paper with black or blue ink. His handwriting was small and fast, hard to read at times. The messaging was clear all the while - I love you, we had a conflict of a big experience, here's why I did what I did, here's how I feel about what you did, here's how I think we can grow. You're important to me and I love you.

The Sting of Exclusion and the Drive for Inclusion
Even with a supportive father figure, I occasionally felt like a piece of a larger puzzle, unsure of exactly how I fit. Family dynamics can be tricky. Step-siblings and extended relatives already had their histories, inside jokes, and established roles. Though everyone was kind, I was acutely aware that I was stitching myself into a quilt that was partly woven long before I arrived.

That sense of being on the outside looking in lingered, igniting in me a fierce drive to ensure others wouldn't feel the way I sometimes did. If you've ever spotted someone standing awkwardly at the edge of a social gathering (or maybe this was you) and felt compelled to wave them over, you understand.

In the early years of my new life in a blended family, I spent a lot of time at my Grandma Lillian's house on the Lewis River north of Portland, sometimes just the two of us on weekends. She was integral for me to carve out special memories where I continued to have plenty of independent time, but also a good deal of structured activities. Lillian was widowed when my Dad and his two older brothers were still quite young, and she raised three boys on her own. During World War II, she was a part of the *Rosie the Riveter* group of women who worked on the Columbia River along the Vancouver, Washington riverbank where they made parts for the Boeing planes that went over to fight the war. She later became a nurse, and then a teacher.

While at her house, as I often was, I would walk down to Lucia Falls, a short but wide and terraced waterfall, about a mile down the secluded riverside path with her. Later, I would walk on my own. I would watch the salmon run every Spring. I paid attention to Grandma Lillian's daily habits. She walked in nature, tended her small garden and flowers, chopped her own wood, boiled alpine river water for drinking atop her wrought iron stove. She kept up with her friends and family via active letter writing, travelled globally, and generally kept things simple.

I picked the mauve-colored, tart salmon berries all summer in the hillside across from her home, and now giggle to myself at the freedom I was allotted in the 1980s and early 1990s. "Watch out for bears", was the guidance before heading out on these adventures. Half of the time my step siblings, Jon and Jenny, were with me, and some of the time, cousins Keith and Kelly, Scot and Jimmy, Kevin and Stephanie would visit from a little farther away and we had a "fort" we built out over the years down along the riverside. It was not structurally sound, but we collectively did our best.

I also remember feeling the pain of exclusion in the first summers we were building the riverside fort. One of my new cousins shouted at me, "you're not allowed in, you're not our REAL cousin!" It stung deeply, the easy cruelty of children.

At school, I started inviting classmates who seemed interesting but lonely to sit with me at lunch and play with me at recess. I tried to use my athletic influence, and my budding height—I was already

5'10" in the 5th grade—for good, so that everyone on the playground got to play, not just the popular kids. Somewhere inside, I made a promise: We're all going together.

During these years, I had discovered an anchor in sports, which grounded me in a world of rules, teamwork, and the exhilarating burn of pushing my body to its limits. Athletics became a channel for my restless and sometimes melancholy energy and a reminder that, no matter what was happening at home or with bullies, I could find structure and community on the playing field. If you've felt that surge of endorphins, the clarity of mind that comes from a hard-fought game, you'll know how it can make the rest of life's uncertainties feel just a bit more manageable.

I slowly and steadily built my own unique community of friendships - other kids from sports, kids from class, friends of friends. Getting to know other families from sports and school. Beth and Julie were girls who eventually became and remained close to me ever since.

Those times of young self-discovery gave me insight of what could be. Sometimes, you don't need a plan. Just a long string of moments to start to paint a picture. A breath that tells the truth before your brain can catch up. Maybe you've had a beginning like that, too—the kind that didn't announce itself, but settled into your bones.

The Soft Opening Into Everything
There's something about your early twenties—the heady mix of freedom, uncertainty, and sheer audacity—that makes you believe you can reinvent yourself at any moment. And honestly? You can.

I did.

After attending Washington State University to study Communications in Media, I came home to the Portland area and rented a house with my friend Julie and our two cats Chloe and Jimi. While it was a cute home and a fine life, I had already been longing for a big change. I had been feeling the pull of depression while dealing with my parents separation when I was in high school, and divorce during my years away at college.

She gave birth to my brother Mitch when I was 15, and looking back, surely she had suffered from postpartum depression. In the mid 90s, this would have hardly been a diagnosed illness. Nonetheless, I remember seeing medications in her bathroom to manage her symptoms. I noticed her drinking white wine during the day, most days of the week. I worried about my baby brother Mitch while I was at school, working at my part time job at Ross Dress for Less, and hanging out with my friends. I often encouraged us all to spend time at my house after school and on the weekends so we could look after him.

My Dad had moved out of the house around the time Mitch was one, and my parents officially separated. My step siblings Jon and Jenny naturally stopped coming over every other weekend. Family vacations were no longer scheduled. My parents bought me a grey 1986 Toyota Camry with low miles and I gained my independence. I filled the missing pieces with my friendships – we threw countless house parties at each of our family homes and took day trips out to the coast. My dear friends Beth and Julie and I went out to countless punk rock shows (our friends were all in bands), and explored the cool late night dining and arts scene in Portland most nights.

So coming home after being away at a big college in a small town 6 hours away felt...untethered. I didn't have fun at school - I was bored. I liked learning but couldn't seem to get a grasp on what my community was. I felt the most connection with the misfits, the artists, the other outsiders. My friends back home seemed to have not missed a beat while continuing their lives. Some had gone and come back like me, others went right into the workforce. A few boyfriends came and went, but what I yearned for the most was a new adventure.

It's a strange thing, to grow up loved but unseen. To be surrounded by familiar voices, school corridors you could navigate blindfolded, grocery store clerks who ask about your grandparents, and yet feel like your most essential self never really had a name in the world you came from.

That was Portland for me. A city of green and gray, art and rain, raspberries and rivers. A place where I became, and a place I quietly outgrew. The edges of me had always felt a little sharper, a little wider, a little less containable than what people expected. I had an itch I couldn't name. A sense that something was waiting for me—but not there. Not in the tidy neighborhoods or predictable weather. Not in the knowing glances from people who thought they had my story memorized.

I had visited some friends in San Diego my Freshman year in college and had a special memory of visiting someone's adorable house in Mission Beach - a quaint and quirky beach neighborhood with pretty pastel houses and apartments, white lights strung everywhere, the salt air prominent with each breath. And it was warm and cool at the same time. The second I arrived, I felt it. The air, the light, the energy. A soft yes moved through my body.

I was disoriented. I had tried on different majors like outfits—curious, eager, but unconvinced. Nothing felt quite right. I remember coming home during breaks, unsure how to answer the question everyone asked: What are you going to do?

But now, I did.

Armed with a few boxes, my friendly cat Jimi, a pile of colorful early 2000s fashion choices, and the certainty that something beautiful was waiting for me, I packed up and drove to San Diego. I'd fallen in love with the sunlit sidewalks of Mission Beach during a college spring break trip, and from that moment on, I knew—bone-deep—I would live there someday. The knowledge wasn't logical. It was spiritual. Just like so many of the decisions that would shape my life to come.

I had finished my studies at Washington State University, and despite a tiny voice whispering that I might want something more holistic, more human, more me, I followed the traditional path—until I didn't. San Diego called, and I listened.

This was still the golden era of Craigslist, when you could find a roommate, a massage table, a used car, and a random DJ for your house party all in the same scroll. I landed a sublet in what I thought was a dreamy beachfront house... until I moved in and realized it was more "bro-zone disaster" than a beach bungalow. Think sticky floors, half-inflated air mattresses, and three college guys who didn't believe in the concept of trash bags. The good news was the guys were all gone home for Summer Break. So, I rolled my sleeves up, got out the cleaning supplies, and turned the nearly beachfront bungalow into my first home in my new city.

The Pacific Ocean was fifty feet from my front door, so I held my breath, (literally, until the house was clean), and chose gratitude. I believed that even this slightly grimy situation was part of something good. I was on my way.

And even though I didn't know exactly where I was going, I felt something new rising in me. Something that said: Trust this.

Best Friend Soul Mate

Love, in its truest form, isn't just the butterflies or the cinematic first encounters—it's the throughline of a life well lived. It's the quiet, daily choice to grow together rather than apart. My love story with my husband of over 20 years, Kaya, has shaped me, steadied me, and lifted me beyond what I ever imagined. It has been passionate, unwavering, and at times tested by the weight of real life. But at the core of it all is a soul-deep connection that neither of us have ever questioned.

I still think back to those early days when we first met at a beach house party, when we found our way to each other and never let go. It wasn't perfect—nothing ever is—but it was easy in the ways that mattered. He quickly became my best friend, my partner, the person who looked at me like I could do no wrong, (even when I most certainly could).

Kaya has always made me feel like every idea, every dream, every wild, half-baked plan I've ever had was worth considering. He listens, really listens, to all the ways my mind runs ahead. He encourages me to explore, to try, to fail if needed—because he knows I will rise. This has been one of the greatest gifts of my life—his ability to love me expansively, without limits, without trying to mold me into something smaller or safer.

But love, no matter how deep, is not immune to the realities of life. We've faced struggles that could have broken us—financial hardships, exhaustion from raising young children, the societal pressures of a mixed-race marriage. And yet, through it all, we have remained unwavering in one thing: the choice to keep choosing each other.

The Challenges of Building a Life Together
Every love story faces its own unique set of challenges. Ours were not insurmountable, but they were real.

We were broke young parents of two babies under 2 years old, stretching every dollar, trying to figure out how to make it all work. Those years were humbling. We learned to create joy in simplicity, to support each other through exhaustion, to find laughter even when stress threatened to swallow us whole.

Neither of us walked into parenthood knowing exactly what to do. We weren't just raising children— we were growing ourselves. We made mistakes. We apologized. We adjusted. And above all, we stayed present.

I'm a white woman, Kaya is a black man. Some of the world has real opinions about interracial love, even today. We've encountered stares, assumptions, and blatant racism. I had to unlearn many things, to listen more than I spoke, to recognize that love alone wasn't enough, and it had to be backed by action, awareness, and advocacy.

Long-term love requires a delicate balance: growing together without losing yourself. Kaya and I have always prioritized each other's individual evolution alongside our growth as a couple. We don't clip each other's wings. We challenge, support, and celebrate the growth in each other, even when it pushes us outside of our comfort zones.

Choosing Each Other, Always

Love is about choice. And in our 20+ years together, Kaya and I have chosen each other again and again, even when things weren't easy. Especially when things weren't easy.

There is a quiet strength in knowing your partner isn't going anywhere. That, even in the midst of challenges, they are in it with you. That they are lifting you up rather than tearing you down. This has been the backbone of our relationship—our ability to communicate, to listen, to adjust, and to keep moving forward.

That's the thing about love—it's about daily commitment, beyond just romance or grand gestures. It's about saying, "I see you, I choose you, and I will keep choosing you," even when life gets messy. And it does get messy. But every time we faced something that could have torn us apart, we circled back to that core vow: we lift each other up. We communicate, we listen, we adjust, and we keep love alive..

Key Takeaways for Navigating Long-Term Love:

· Prioritize Communication: Assumptions destroy relationships. We have built a habit of checking in with each other, even about the small things.

· Commit to Growth—Together and Individually: Stagnation is the death of passion. We've always encouraged each other to evolve.

· Find Joy in Simplicity: Love is built in the small moments—the coffee made in the morning, the hand on your back after a long day, the inside jokes that no one else understands.

· Never Stop Choosing Each Other: Passion fades if

you let it. Love deepens when you actively nurture it.

Parenting with Love and Intention
Parenting with Kaya has been a reflection of the lessons we learned in our own childhoods: that care, consistency, and a willingness to grow matter more than sheer perfection. We decided early on that our children, Yasira and Atreju, would never be an afterthought. They'd be the center of our home, the impetus for our evolution, the reason we refuse to settle for anything less than we can be.

What I didn't know was that I was preparing for motherhood all those years I spent in my grandfather's greenhouse, or when I was welcoming the new siblings my stepfather brought into my life. But looking back, I see how those experiences primed me for a love so expansive it could cradle an entire family. Each of us grows alongside the others, forging a dynamic, living tapestry of support and trust.

I didn't know I wanted to be a mother until a few days before I became pregnant with Yasira. I had just turned 25, and a wave of knowing washed over me one day while I was at home relaxing. I felt her presence near me, and suddenly I was ready to have a baby. Once that energetic shift happened, I stepped into it fully. Kaya and I were pregnant within a week. I knew my girl was coming.

I wanted to be fully present—not just physically, but emotionally, mentally, spiritually. I wanted them to see what self-love and self-respect looked like so they could embody it themselves.

And Kaya, from the very beginning, understood the importance of that. He encouraged me to take care of myself, to pursue my dreams, to never lose my sense of identity. He has always been my biggest supporter in self-growth, and that, in turn, has made me a better mother, wife, and person.

When Yasira turned 1, we knew it was time to bring our next precious family member into our world. This time, the feeling was grounded, solid, sure. Our special boy Atreju came 9 months later, big and sweet.

Yasira and Atreju have been our greatest teachers, our mirrors, our heart-walking-outside-of-our-bodies. They are beautiful, hilarious, sharp, kind, curious, and independent. Watching them grow into themselves has been the greatest privilege of my life.

Parenting Lessons We've Learned Along the Way:

· Be Present: You don't have to be a perfect parent. You just have to show up, again and again.

· Foster Independence: We have always encouraged our children to think for themselves, to question, to explore.

· Lead by Example: Kids don't learn from what you say. They learn from what they see.

Mixed-Race Love: Growth, Awareness, and Advocacy

Kaya and I have navigated additional layers to our story. Being a white woman married to a Black man has exposed us to cultural assumptions, biases, and, at times, blatant racism. While our bond has always felt rock-solid to us, the world around us doesn't always make it easy. We've learned that true love means being willing to stand up for one another—not just in private, but in public spaces where preconceived notions about race and identity can stir conflict or misunderstanding.

Our children, Yasira and Atreju, inhabit two cultural worlds. We've tried to ensure they feel at home in both, teaching them to stand tall in their identities.

Our love story might seem "unconventional" from the outside, but to us, it's simply ours. And it's taught me a deeper empathy, an understanding that sometimes belonging means crafting a space of your own when the world won't hand it to you.

Realizing my own blind spots was a humbling process. Love alone isn't enough to shield someone from systemic realities. I had to educate myself, to listen to Kaya and his immediate family's experiences, to recognize my own privilege and how that affected our children.

Have you ever been in a relationship that compelled you to see the world through someone else's eyes, to the point where you're changed forever? That's what it's been like for me. It's been an evolution—sometimes uncomfortable, always enlightening, and absolutely worth every awkward conversation or societal misstep.

The world has opinions about interracial love, even now. The looks, the assumptions, the small (and not-so-small) moments of racism we've encountered—they're real. But they've never shaken us. If anything, they've strengthened our bond and our resolve.

This journey has made me a better, more thoughtful person. It has made me more intentional in every aspect of my life. Love is love, but love is also action, growth, and the willingness to evolve.

The Lessons I've Learned:

1. Love Alone Isn't Enough – Love doesn't erase societal realities. I had to actively educate myself and be willing to have difficult conversations. My family was far away, while Kaya's family was deeply rooted in a mostly Black community. It took time for me to understand certain cultural nuances, to recognize that my experience wasn't universal. There were moments where I felt like an outsider at first, not because I wasn't welcomed, but because I had learning to do.

2. Parenting Mixed-Race Kids Requires Intentionality – Raising children who exist in two worlds means making sure they feel at home in both. We've always prioritized open conversations about identity, about race, about what it means to move through the world in their skin. We wanted them to be proud of every part of who they are.

3. Allyship Is a Verb – It's about continuous learning and action. It's not about getting it right all the time,

but about being committed to doing better.

4. We Define Our Own Narrative – The world has its opinions, but our love is ours. And that has always been enough.

5. Understanding Privilege and Bias – I've had to recognize my own privilege and the ways unconscious bias plays out in everyday life. It's been a journey of sitting down, shutting up, and listening—of realizing that love alone isn't enough; action and awareness are required too.

Reflection and Action: Applying These Lessons to Your Own Life

1. What does "choosing love" look like for you? In relationships, love is a daily choice. How do you show up for your partner, your family, your community?

2. Are you fostering growth in yourself and your relationships? Stagnation leads to resentment. Where can you support and encourage personal evolution—both in yourself and your loved ones?

3. How intentional are you about the narratives you pass down to your children? Our kids absorb everything. What values are you modeling for them?

4. Are you committed to seeing and understanding perspectives beyond your own? Growth requires humility. What blind spots might you need to address?

___

Love, real love, is not passive. It is active, intentional, and evolving. It is the foundation on which we build a life—not the fairy tale, but the real, enduring, soul-deep connection that makes everything else possible.

Enduring Love
Kaya and I built a life around our love, and from that foundation, we became parents to two incredible kids—Yasira and Atreju—each of them uniquely themselves, but both embodying the very best of us. Becoming a mother wasn't something I planned, but the moment it happened, I knew it was right. I knew them before I met them. And because of them, I have always been driven to become the best version of myself.

Our family has been the heartbeat of everything Kaya and I have built together. We chose an intentional, community-centered, beachy lifestyle, where our children could grow up surrounded by love, adventure, and the kind of freedom that allows a person to truly know themselves. We didn't come into parenthood with all the answers—no one does—but we were present, and we were willing to grow alongside them.

The Invitation That Opened Everything
A few years before Kaya and I were becoming parents, I was still waiting tables at Olive Garden, and had settled into my new beach lifestyle. It had been my steady paycheck through college, and now, it was my bridge to something new—even if I didn't know what that something was yet. And as anyone

who's ever worked in service knows, you learn a lot about people when you bring them never-ending breadsticks.

That's where I met her—one of the first new friends I made in San Diego. She had soft eyes, the kind of voice that made you lean in, and a grounded confidence that made me curious.

"You're not from here, are you?" she asked one afternoon as we rolled silverware together.

"Nope, I just landed."

"I knew it. You feel different. Are you a massage therapist?"

I laughed. "I'm not. Should I be?"

"You should," she said, smiling. "I'm starting massage school in a couple of weeks. You should come to the open house."

I didn't know what compelled me to say yes. Aside from my newfound beach lifestyle, my plan was to utilize my college education in Communications and Media and find work in my field. But something in her energy—and something in me—nudged forward.

Go.

That single moment—the way she said it, the way I felt when she said it—changed my life. I didn't know then what it meant to follow an invitation like that. I do now. Sometimes the door opens gently. You just have to be ready to notice.

The Day Everything Clicked
A few weeks later, I went to the open house.

By my early twenties, I was ready for something that combined my passion for nurturing others with the practical need to earn a living. I'd always been drawn to the idea of helping people feel cared for— physically, mentally, emotionally, and spiritually. So when that coworker at Olive Garden mentioned a local school of holistic healing arts (affectionately known as SOHARTS), something clicked.

Stepping through those doors felt like walking into the next evolution of my grandfather's greenhouse: a sanctuary of growth, except this time for people's well-being rather than plants. Soft music, the scent of essential oils, shelves lined with books on massage, reflexology, and energy work—it was equal parts enchanting and intimidating. But deep down, I sensed: This is the place where all my scattered interests come together.

The School of Healing Arts—SOHARTS, as we lovingly called it—was tucked into an unassuming building, but the moment I stepped through the front door I felt a sense of being enveloped. Seen. Recalled to something I didn't even know I'd forgotten.

It smelled like incense and herbs and love. There were bowls of Trader Joe's cookies on mismatched platters, smiling people wearing linen pants and essential oil blends. It was intimate and quirky and infused with intention. I'd never seen anything like it. But my body said, *stay*.

The tour was a blur of treatment rooms, classrooms, and people speaking in the soft tones of those who have nothing to prove. A faculty member handed me a brochure about their 1,000-hour holistic health practitioner program and I nodded politely, though I had no idea what it really entailed.

By the end of the visit, I found myself saying words I didn't expect:

"Do you have financial aid?"

What happened next still feels like divine choreography. Within weeks, I was accepted into the program—and granted a full-ride work-study scholarship. It felt like the universe put a hand on my back and whispered: "This way, love."

There was no turning back.

Your beginning might look nothing like mine. But it matters. The early mess, the strange jobs, the friendships, the questions—they're not detours. They're clues. What shaped you that still whispers to you now?

The Soft Cult (Kind Of)
Let's get this out of the way: my dad—practical, consistent, thoughtful—eventually asked me if I had joined a cult. In his defense, I did wear all white on Thursdays, lit candles during class, and bowed at the beginning and end of our sessions. The reverence was real.

But if this was a cult, it was the gentlest one imaginable. No one asked me to abandon my family or hand over my life savings. What they did ask was that I show up as a student of life. To listen more deeply.

To question gently. To feel things I had spent years trying not to feel.

For the first time, I was in a room full of people who wanted to be there. We weren't earning credits. We were answering a higher call.

And I was obsessed.

Falling in Love with the Healing Arts
Our classes were deep and weird and wildly transformative. We studied Zen Touch Shiatsu, Thai energy work, macrobiotic nutrition, craniosacral therapy, body reading, facial reading, and the five elements of Traditional Chinese Medicine. I was learning to decode people's physical and emotional patterns. To trace tension to its emotional root. To see beauty in even the most tangled energy.

My work-study hours meant cleaning bathrooms at night, but I didn't care. I was soaking up a new language. And I was good at it. I could feel it. My hands knew things. I'd work on someone during class, and their body would tremble, release, sometimes weep. It was like their pain had just been waiting for permission to leave.

I didn't have the clinical language for it yet, but I

knew I could hold space for people. And that space could be sacred.

Healing isn't polite. It's not always serene or linear. Sometimes, it's loud, holy chaos. Sometimes, it's cleaning bathrooms at night while quietly building your future in the in-between. What part of your life looked like sacrifice, but turned out to be sacred?

The Obsession That Became a Gift
At first, I was just a fascinated student.

But soon, I realized I had a gift. I could read bodies. I could see tension before someone said a word. I could predict where pain would land just by watching someone walk.

I started treating the world like a case study. Standing in line at the grocery store, I'd observe posture. Walking through Pacific Beach crowds, I'd catch the subtle hunch in someone's shoulders and wonder what heartache they carried. I couldn't stop. It wasn't judgment—it was awe. The body was a story waiting to be heard.

I read books on anatomy and energy medicine like they were romance novels. I attended workshops I couldn't afford but volunteered in exchange for entry. I attended small hiking groups through Mission Trails, where the herbalist teacher would point out native plants that could soothe wounds or calm nerves. The more I learned, the more I wanted to learn.

It was like I had fallen into a well of endless wisdom and opportunity to grow. And I didn't want to come up for air.

Have you also been lucky enough to find a place that allowed you to be yourself? A place where your gifts could rise to the surface? What did that place look like? What would those gifts be? I invite you to pay attention to your surroundings. Sometimes our greatest gifts can come from unexpected, simple places.

Beauty Beneath the Surface
Around the same time, my love of beauty deepened.

I'd always loved skincare—serums, masks, rituals, but now, I saw beauty as something different. Something vibrational. I started to notice that people glowed differently when they felt seen. That skin looked luminous when the nervous system was calm. That digestion, sleep, and emotional wellbeing mattered just as much as eye cream.

Beauty, to me, became the outward reflection of what was happening inside.

It wasn't about perfection. It was about vitality. Radiance. Aliveness.

Once I completed my program, I started blending the two—healing and beauty. I'd offer bodywork sessions that included facial massage and hydrosol mist. I'd guide people on personalized nervous system health and suggest herbs for skin clarity. I was mixing the sacred and the sensual, the mystical and the tangible. And it made sense. It made me.

This was where my work started to feel less like a job and more like a calling.

Chosen Family, Found
And then—something even more magical happened.

I started to find my people.

At SOHARTS, and through the wellness circles that spiraled out from it, I met some of the most extraordinary women of my life. Healers, artists, rebels, caregivers. People who didn't need you to be anything other than real. We formed a pack. A chosen family.

It wasn't official, of course. There were no declarations or group contracts. Just a steady rhythm of potlucks, impromptu dance parties, full moon beach and mountain hikes, and mornings spent barefoot in backyards sipping herbal infusions like they were mimosas.

We called each other in. Held each other through heartbreaks. Celebrated every brave yes.

It was wild and soft, nourishing and electric. For the first time since I'd left Portland, I felt home.

SOHARTS became the container for my deeper transformation. I enrolled at the School of Healing Arts not knowing what, exactly, I was signing up for—but I knew it felt right. The school itself was nestled right in the middle of Pacific Beach, surrounded by cafes, boho shops and boutique fitness studios, with the scent of sage and salt air greeting you at the door. It wasn't just a training ground. It was a portal to the new life I had built.

We studied massage, breathwork, energy healing, anatomy, ethics, and client communication. But we also studied ourselves. We learned how to hold space, how to be quiet when someone cried, how to feel without fixing. It was there that I learned how to be with discomfort—my own and others'. That skill would become essential later in my work, long before I called it consulting.

SOHARTS—The School of Healing Arts—became my anchor.

I had enrolled not fully knowing what I was signing up for, only that every part of me said yes when I walked through those doors. The school was nestled into a quiet corner of Pacific Beach, and from the moment you entered, the air felt different. Salt and sage. Rose oil and lavender. It wasn't sterile, like other massage schools I'd visited. It was warm. Welcoming. Like someone had intentionally made the space feel sacred.

We studied a wide range of modalities—massage therapy, breathwork, anatomy, ethics, energy reading, therapeutic communication. But we also studied ourselves. Our patterns. Our projections. Our pain. We weren't taught to fix people—we were taught to be with them. To create enough safety and presence that healing could emerge naturally.

That was the first time I realized: This is what I've always done. This is what I'm here to do.

I wasn't just learning to press on tissue. I was learning how to listen with my whole body.

The First Public Client—and the First Breakdown
One of the first clients I ever worked on during clinic hours changed everything. They were a woman in her 40s, quiet, visibly tense. I was nervous. I wanted to get it right. But the moment I placed my hands on her shoulders, they burst into tears. Not polite tears—wailing. Her whole body convulsed with grief.

I froze for a moment. Every part of me screamed, "Fix it. Stop it. Say something."

But instead, I did something I hadn't known I was capable of yet. I stayed. I didn't rush. I didn't over-explain. I didn't try to make it neat. I just breathed. Softened my grip. Let my palms become a place for that grief to land.

That moment taught me something I've never forgotten: People don't just want to be helped. They want to be witnessed.

That was the seed. And it would grow into a forest. Luckily my teacher witnessed this experience and brought it to the class for discussion. "You're an empath", she said. "Let's talk about it..." and she went on to describe to us at great length, the science on energetic exchange and release, and how to work with it, not hold on to it, and channel an opening for healing through the pain people hold.

I went on to have several other powerful and key experiences while in school, and was grateful for my teachers to show me how to develop and deepen boundaries and personal power to stay healthy.

This chapter of my life was a *re-wilding*. A return to myself. A sacred YES to everything I hadn't known how to name before. Beauty. Belonging. Intuition. The power of community. And the quiet but profound realization that healing doesn't always look like progress—it often looks like pausing.

I had successfully and happily completed over 1200 hours of classes in my initial Holistic Health Practitioner program—reflexology, bodywork techniques, aromatherapy, herbology, nutrition—soaking up everything I could about how to facilitate relaxation and healing. And yet, I was struck by the fact that many of my classmates were profoundly gifted in the healing arts, yet struggled to see how these gifts could translate into viable businesses that could support them financially. Wasn't the point, I wondered, to bring these healing modalities to as many people as possible?

That's when I realized that wellness and business don't have to be opposing forces. They can be two sides of the same coin. A thriving wellness venture could employ more healers, reach more clients, and build supportive communities around the globe—if only the people with these gifts would embrace the idea of entrepreneurship. This epiphany planted the seed of my future career in luxury wellness business, an arena I never thought I'd enter, but which soon became the perfect meeting point for my talents and curiosity.

* * *

I left SOHARTS with a certificate, yes. But more than that, I left with clarity. I was never meant to work in traditional media, like I thought I would. I was meant to hold space. To translate energy. To build beauty. And to walk beside others as they uncovered the parts of themselves they'd forgotten.

It was the first yes. The beginning of a long line of intuitive decisions that didn't always make sense—but always made me.

3

Running With Wolves

Running With Wolves: When Home Isn't a Place, But a People

If you're the woman who's built success by being everything to everyone else, this chapter is yours. It's about friendships that hold you when the world forgets to, and the freedom of finally being seen without performance.

"We weren't trying to be good. We were trying to be free. And we found that freedom in each other."

When I left the Pacific Northwest in my early twenties, it wasn't just a move. It was a departure from everything familiar, a self-initiation into the unknown. I didn't bring a community with me when I packed up my life and drove down to San Diego. I came alone—with a cat, a car, and a dream of living by the beach.

And even though the sunshine and ocean air felt like a promise, there were moments that first year when I felt like a castaway on the sand. I had to rebuild everything. I had to figure out who I was outside the context of people who'd known me forever. There was freedom in that. And fear, too.

So I did what I've always done when things felt uncertain: I moved my body. I walked the winding trails around Mission Bay and Ocean Beach, jogged the boardwalks while reveling in the scent of sunscreen in the air, rode my bike up hills just to feel the push of wind in my lungs. And I swam in the ocean daily in the warmer months. Tried to surf—badly. But I kept returning to it all. To the water. To the movement. To myself.

I spent many days walking San Diego's delightful Balboa Park's paths alone with my journal in hand, and feeling the subtle tug of a new kind of belonging, not to a place or a person, but to myself. The new pace of life I had been creating felt exhilarating, vibrant, and refreshing. My idea years before about going to Southern California to revel in the sun had proven to be a wonderful decision.

Slowly, through that rhythm of showing up, I began to meet more people. People who were also figuring themselves out. People who were willing to ask hard questions. People who didn't need a history to love you well.

What I didn't expect was how quickly I would find the ones who felt like a soul family.

Three of my soul sisters, Drea, Aysun, and Christy, make my heart full to this day. We did everything together, new moon potlucks, foraging hikes, long talks under the stars at the beach. We cooked barefoot in shared kitchens and sat on living room floors laughing until our faces hurt, while Temple of India Incense burned on a nearby side table. We made up holidays just to celebrate each other. There was a sense of being completely myself in that circle. A kind of chosen family energy that still brings tears to my eyes when I think about it.

We were young and tender and fierce. We cheered

for each other, challenged each other, and healed together. These weren't surface friendships, they were the kind you build your life around. The kind that shapes who you become.

I studied massage, breathwork, energy healing, nutrition, herbs, anatomy, ethics, and communication with the intention to serve others. But I also studied myself. I learned how to hold space, how to be quiet when someone cried, how to feel without fixing. It was there that I learned how to be with discomfort, my own and others'. That skill would become essential later in my work, long before I knew what it was.

Outside of class, we built our own rituals. Morning tea in silence. Writing sessions. Beach days where we pulled tarot cards and shared dreams. An and I used to make flower bundles for each other on hard days. We knew how to offer beauty without needing to fix anything. That's sacred friendship.

There was also a camping trip in Julian I'll never forget. A group of us had gone into the woods to disconnect and reset. One night, we saw glowing orbs, literal orbs of light, floating above us in the trees. Some people were fascinated, others were terrified. A few left early the next morning, unsettled. But those of us who stayed? We stayed on purpose. We wanted to understand. To be in the mystery. That night reminded me that the unknown isn't something to fear, it's something to explore.

There are moments the world splits, before and after. Seen and unseen. And you get to decide: stay grounded, or trust the mystery. What have you witnessed that others didn't believe... but you couldn't forget?

It was a return to myself. A sacred YES to everything I hadn't known how to name before. Beauty. Belonging. Intuition. The power of community. And the quiet but profound realization that healing doesn't always look like progress, it often looks like pausing.

I left SOHARTS with a certificate, yes. But more than that, I left with clarity. I was never meant to be in traditional media. I was meant to hold space. To translate energy. To build beauty. And to walk beside others as they uncovered the parts of themselves they'd forgotten.

It was the first yes. The beginning of a long line of intuitive decisions that didn't always make sense, but always made me.

The Slow Build of Belonging

The first person who truly became mine in this new world was An.

I met her at SOHARTS, she was further along in her program when I started mine, and I remember spotting her in an advanced massage class. She had this magnetic, effortlessly cool energy, earthy and wise, but sharp in all the best ways. We didn't talk much at first, but I noticed her. People like An are hard not to notice.

Eventually, she and her husband came to a poetry night Kaya and I were hosting at our East Village rental. It was one of those small, scrappy gatherings, candles melted onto mismatched platters, thrifted pillows on the floor, everyone bringing a poem, a guitar, a bottle, or a story. I remember sitting on the stoop that night as the evening settled into laughter and verses and thinking, Oh. These are my people.

An felt it too. That quiet click of friendship. That unspoken yes.

From there, things expanded like vines, slow and strong. An introduced me to Carla. I met the three Jennys. Then came Jessica, Heather, Najah, Gaby, and the rest of the wild and wonderful wolf pack that would become my chosen family. It was like the universe had waited for me to arrive before revealing this particular constellation of humans.

Each introduction came with a feeling of recognition, like I'd known them already in some other lifetime. And while everyone was so different, diverse cultural and economic backgrounds, ages, aesthetics, there was an invisible thread stitching us together. We were women who didn't mind the mess. Women who asked big questions over green juice or red wine. Women who believed in healing and in laughing until we cried. There was no need to posture or impress. We showed up as ourselves, and that was enough.

Carla had a dry, brutally honest sense of humor that cut straight through your nonsense in the best way. She was the first person to tell me I was doing too much, and somehow made it sound like love. She also had (and still has) a soft spot the size of the moon for senior rescue dogs. There was always one, sometimes ten, in her orbit, sleeping on her lap or riding shotgun in her Prius. She never made a big deal about it, but she quietly lived the values we all shared: take care of what others forget to love.

Jenny had this intuitive depth I felt instantly. She

remembered the small things. She'd text me days after a passing comment and say, "I found that book you mentioned," or "I saw this and thought of you." She had a way of noticing people. Jessica was the same, bright, tender, artistic, and soulfully rooted in a way that felt like a breath of fresh air.

Heather and I often met at her house for breakfast - a simple toasted sourdough avocado toast, a free range fried egg, followed by a workout and long one-on-one talks. These weekday hang sessions fed my soul as the kids grew through their early elementary school years and I learned to consistently carve time out for myself. And Gaby with her soulful brown eyes, the greatest empathetic listener I've known.

Our friendships were about presence. You could disappear for a few weeks and come back to open arms, a hot meal, and someone asking, "Okay, where are we really at today?"

There's a particular kind of grace that happens when you're seen without being explained. These women offered me that again and again.

We Were the Circle
Our group wasn't a club. It wasn't curated or hierarchical. It was more like a garden, growing

organically, tended by love, humor, and deep mutual respect. We didn't need to perform for each other. We just... showed up.

Our gatherings weren't flashy. They were held in backyards, on patios, inside cozy homes filled with kids, dogs, incense, potluck meals, and music playing low in the background. There was always an open door. Always a place on the couch. Always someone who had your back without needing to be asked.

There was a restful rhythm to the way we did life together. Carla, who was deeply involved in geriatric and last-chance dog rescue, always had a new pup in tow, or in her lap. By association, we were all part of that mission. We laughed about it, but we also took it seriously. When a creature needed a home, one of us would usually step up. We saw rescue as a collective act, not just for animals, but for each other.

We built rituals into the everyday. Morning beach walks followed by tea and honey. Clothing swaps and avocado toast. Shared meals where someone brought gluten-free vegan cupcakes and someone else brought six bottles of wine. There was a rhythm, but no script.

I was the only one in the group who eventually had two babies when we first started hanging out. Later, we added another Jenny (yes, there were multiple), and Jessica too, who had little kids. We quickly fell into a rhythm of raising our kids side-by-side. We would swap stories about teething and tantrums while passing babies between arms and roasting vegetables in our kitchens.

Sometimes we parented collectively, taking turns holding space when someone was overwhelmed, celebrating small wins like a full night's sleep or a successful nap transfer. We didn't act like it was revolutionary. It just made sense. This was village life, rebuilt on the bones of our longing.

We traveled together. Camping trips in Southern California, impromptu getaways to Mexico, even longer adventures to places like India. Some trips included kids, spouses, and dogs; others were just us women, reconnecting with ourselves and each other in places where the air felt thin with possibility. I remember one trip where Najah led us through a nighttime meditation on the beach, all of us wrapped in shawls, salt wind in our hair, breathing with the moon. We weren't just friends, we were kin.

It wasn't just the events or locations that made it

sacred. It was the consistency. The way we could rely on each other. The way we trusted each other with the tender parts of life, divorces, illness, fertility struggles, career pivots, family dynamics. We held all of it, always with one hand on truth and one hand on humor.

That was the magic: We could go from sobbing to howling with laughter in five minutes flat. Our jokes were sharp, dry, and sarcastic. But beneath every punchline was a knowing: You are safe here. We love you just as you are.

Sometimes I think about how rare that is, not just to be loved, but to be loved as is. To be celebrated not for your polish, but for your process. We never had a friendship contract, but if we had, it would've read: "You can be messy here. You can be magic here. You can be in-between here. Just don't ghost the group text."

Where Loyalty and Laughter Live
We didn't always say it out loud, but we knew: this was rare.

To be so deeply known and still so easily loved. To be held accountable and still free to grow. To be surrounded by sharp, creative, ambitious women who didn't ask you to shrink or prove yourself, but who expected you to show up fully, mess and all.

There were nights we stayed up too late talking about heartbreak, about parents getting older, about dreams we were scared to speak aloud. There were texts at midnight and drop-offs of soup and herbal tinctures and moon-charged crystals. We shared everything: books, playlists, favorite eye creams, psychic downloads, and the kind of advice that you don't write in journals, you carry it in your bones.

The humor was always there. That dry, quick-witted, nobody's-taking-themselves-too-seriously humor that could crack through any tension. Especially with An. After we'd been apart for a while and finally reunited, the jokes and bits would just flow like they'd never left the room. Every time, I'd catch myself thinking, Damn, I'm funny, and not in a self-congratulatory way. In a *these people make me more myself* kind of way.

That's what this tribe did for me. They reflected back my own expansion. They held a mirror to my best self and invited her to stay.

And if you're reading this wondering if that kind of friendship is still possible... whether you've outgrown your old circle or feel like everyone's already found their people, I want you to know: it is. These relationships weren't born from ease or perfect timing. They were born from presence. From staying in the room. From choosing to care, even when life got busy or messy or hard.

We all brought something to the circle. Unique flavors, perspectives, and rhythms. Some were more business-minded, others deeply spiritual. Some were artists, some entrepreneurs, some parents, some partners. But the unifying thread was our collective openness to growth. We were women who said yes to becoming, over and over again.

And in that becoming, we learned from each other. Supported each other. Called each other up, not out. I noticed what each woman excelled at and asked, how can I learn from her? That respect was never performative. It was woven into our DNA as a group.

We didn't always agree. But we always cared.

And if you're seeking that kind of care, that kind of closeness, maybe this is your invitation to start building it. Slowly. Honestly. Without needing it to look like anyone else's circle. Start with one person. Or maybe start with yourself.

Belonging by Design

Looking back now, I can see how intentional I was, sometimes unconsciously, sometimes deliberately, about building the kind of community I'd longed for as a child. One where everyone felt invited. Where inclusion wasn't a concept but a practiced way of being. Where there was room for the quiet ones, the messy ones, the late-blooming ones.

I had felt like an outsider at different points in my life. Not always, but enough to notice. Enough to remember what it felt like to not quite belong. So when I stepped into adulthood, I became the architect of something different. Something deeply inclusive. Something that allowed people to exhale and be.

And I brought that intention into every friendship, every group hang, every weekend trip, every text thread that turned into a sacred lifeline. I didn't want to create a hierarchy of closeness. I wanted us all to go together.

It was emotional, yes, but it was also strategic. I was testing ideas, even then. Watching what made people feel safe enough to open up. What created longevity in relationships. What kinds of rituals built real intimacy. I didn't have a name for it back then, but this was the early foundation of what would later become the favorite elements of my life's work: designing experiences, environments, and businesses where people could feel more like themselves.

That mindset of radical togetherness became the blueprint for how I built my brand, my business, and my leadership style. It's why I've always believed in collaboration over competition. It's why I listen before I lead. It's why I prioritize psychological safety in every room I facilitate.

And if you're a leader, a founder, or someone in any position of influence, know this: community doesn't happen by accident. Culture is curated. It's cultivated through every tone you set, every pause you take, every generous decision you make when nobody's watching.

Those years in San Diego taught me you don't need a childhood connection to create lifelong bonds. You need presence. You need reciprocity. You need the courage to let people see you before you've figured everything out.

I didn't become the woman I am because I was ready. I became her because I found people who believed in her before she even showed up. And if you're still becoming, still unraveling, still healing, still trying to trust your voice, this chapter is your reminder. You're not behind. You're on the edge of something sacred.

Find your wolves. The ones who won't let you shrink. The ones who see your power, even when you forget. Life's too short for small talk and shallow applause.

The Soul of the Circle
These friendships weren't just emotional support. They were emotional expansion. They made me more curious, more creative, more courageous. Some friends challenged me in business. Others opened my heart in ways I didn't know it needed opening. A few made me laugh so hard I swear they added years to my life.

I started seeing each relationship as a mirror, showing me a part of myself I was meant to remember. And I paid attention. I invested. I gave as much as I received, and explored how much more I could give. Because that's the currency of real friendship: attention, presence, and the willingness to hold space for evolution.

These women knew me when I was still becoming,

as I stumbled, wandered, and occasionally found myself stranded. And they didn't flinch.

They reminded me that community isn't a luxury, it's a life force. It's a form of healing that can't be replicated in isolation. That shared meals and shared grief and shared celebration are all part of the same medicine.

And this is what I want to offer you, dear reader:

A reminder that you don't have to do this alone. Whether you're building a business, healing a heartbreak, or finding your voice, your circle is out there. And maybe you haven't met them yet. Or maybe you're the one meant to create it.

You don't need a ten-year plan. You don't need a table full of perfect women who never let their mascara run. You just need one real conversation. One invitation. One moment where you dare to say, "I'm in it right now. And I could use a witness."

Ask yourself:
- Who sees the real me?
- Who do I feel most like myself around?
- How can I be the kind of friend I most needed growing up?

And if the answers feel unclear, just start with this: be somewhere honest. Be somewhere nourishing. Be around people who make you laugh so hard you forget to hide your joy.

That's where it begins. Because you don't have to have it all figured out to be loved.

You just have to be willing to show up, and let your wolves find you.

Think about your current relationships—do they reflect your becoming, or your past survival mode? What rituals could you introduce to anchor those friendships into the future?

4

The Business of Being Well

"Holding space was my first gift in business. Building spaces came next."
Work that heals isn't soft. It's strategic. And it's what the next era of leadership will be built on.
This was me standing in my power. Not loud. Not over-explaining. Just clear. And grounded.

When the Student Becomes the Space Holder

When people ask how I became an advisor in the luxury wellness space, I never say, "I planned it." Because I didn't. I lived it. I said yes before I had the full picture. I followed the breadcrumbs of curiosity, beauty, and healing until I realized I had built something intentional, effective, and deeply intuitive.

But long before the strategy, there was practice.

My early days at SOHARTS weren't glamorous. Sure, the air smelled like eucalyptus and there were always plates of Trader Joe's cookies at events—but there was also a lot of scrubbing. Literally. As part of my full-ride work-study scholarship, I regularly cleaned bathrooms at night and mopped studio floors between classes. I wore all white in our Zen Touch Shiatsu program. I rolled up towels until my hands ached. I made herbal tea for colleagues and passed out handouts to new students who were just as wide-eyed as I'd once been.

It was sacred and unfiltered. Grounded and a little unhinged. And I loved it.

Somewhere between Zen Touch Shiatsu and Reiki, between body reading and full moon ceremonies, I started to realize I wasn't just learning technique—I was learning how to listen. How to track people's patterns. How to make someone feel safe enough to soften. That was the real work.

Have you ever been in a season of quiet work? The kind that no one sees, but you know is shaping you? Sometimes the most powerful things we build happen while no one's watching.

Becoming the Therapist People Remembered

I poured myself into the craft over the years. I wasn't trying to become the best, I just couldn't get enough. Every textbook, every continuing education class, every herbal remedy workshop and anatomy deep dive felt like it held another golden thread. I was fascinated by the way people carried stress and how healing could be physical and emotional, all at once. It was like reading poetry written in muscle fibers and energy fields.

And I started to notice something: people were having big experiences on my table. Not every time, but often enough to make my mentors raise their eyebrows and say, "You have the gift."

It scared me a little. What did it mean to have "the gift"? Was I supposed to do something more with it? Was it okay to just be with it? Have you ever had a moment that asked you to choose between comfort and curiosity?

That's when I started asking for more help, from my mentors, from visiting healers, and from the wise women in my life who had seen more than I had. I wanted to keep helping people... without burning myself out. I needed tools for boundaries. Tools for sacred listening. Tools for not absorbing every tear, every trauma, every heavy thing that walked through the door.

What I learned was this: I wasn't there to heal people. I was there to remind them they could heal themselves.

That reframe changed everything.

From Healing Hands to Strategic Mind

Eventually, I began to see patterns, not just in bodies, but in people's behaviors, in their stuck places, in what they believed was possible for their lives. I would ask gentle but direct questions at the end of a session: "What's one small thing you can do this week to feel more grounded?" "What would ease look like for you right now?" "If you felt better, what would you be doing differently?"

I didn't know it at the time, but I was helping them create SMART plans, Specific, Measurable, Achievable, Relevant, Time-bound goals. Not in the stiff, corporate way. In the soft, soul-aligned way. In the way that made healing feel less like an escape and more like a choice.

Without realizing it, I was moving from practitioner to strategist. From service provider to partner in transformation.

And people responded.

They told their friends. They came back. They wrote tearful letters of gratitude. They called me their "healer," their "guide," their "teacher."

It was never just about the massage or energy work.

Have you ever developed something just because your soul asked you to, and then realized it changed everything? That's the beauty of creating from truth. It has a way of drawing the right people in.

Learning the Business from the Inside Out

The deeper I got into the healing arts, the more I wanted to understand what made a wellness business actually work. I'd seen enough to know that talent alone wasn't enough. That beautiful branding didn't guarantee a good experience. That even the most sacred spaces could fall apart without systems, leadership, and intention behind the scenes.

I had spent years honing my craft, from working

in a beach wellness center, to an upscale Aveda Day Spa, to beautiful luxury resorts. Quietly over 10,000 hours of hands-on practical experience came and went, and I had become an expert practitioner in the blink of an eye. When I landed a role at a new luxury property downtown, I found myself involved in one of the favorite and most organized spa teams I've experienced, to this day. I loved my team, and my boss Jennifer. I learned that Jennifer, like many other spa directors, was a massage therapist first. Having two toddlers at home and a burning desire to learn, grow, and succeed, I realized I had more opportunities than I initially thought.

After about a year working here, I asked Jennifer if she would help me develop into management. She not only agreed, but brought the full power of the corporate leadership program to support me. For a full year, she met with me every Wednesday at 10am for an hour. She guided me through the leadership development program, put me through the paces from the ground up, all while I maintained my massage therapy shifts. It was tight for me to get it all done all while the kids were at preschool. They had to be dropped off and picked up within a strict window of time. I was literally on the clock to make it all happen.

That experience taught me the back end of the business: operations, staffing, guest flow, financials, scheduling, service design, and above all, what it meant to create sustainable systems that empowered a team rather than drained them.

Soon, I was no longer just giving treatments. I was influencing the culture of the spa and hotel. I was shaping how teams would communicate, how leaders made decisions, how guests felt the moment they stepped into the space.

Over the next few years, I made my way through the ranks of leadership in luxury resorts and eventually was recruited to what would be a life changing spa director role. There was so much opportunity and change needed to happen at this location. I relished the challenges and adored seeing my efforts pay off in the much improved employee engagement scores, in the increased local guest spend, and with exciting PR and media collaborations where I would, enthusiastically, speak about wellness. And yet again, I was grateful to have a wonderful leader in my Hotel Manager. She guided me through maximizing profits, earning bonuses, and kindly yet firmly cultivating strong professional boundaries, even in the breakneck pace hospitality requires.

Eventually, the ownership group of the hotel approached me with a question that would change my trajectory forever: "Would you consider doing some spa consulting work for us on the side?"

It wasn't something I'd sought out. It wasn't something I even knew I was ready for. But I said *yes*. Because something in me was ready. And so began the next evolution of my career. Not with a business plan or a perfectly polished pitch deck, but with curiosity, care, and a willingness to solve the problems right in front of me.

Some parts of us know the way forward long before the mind can catch up. Whether it shows up in dreams, in signs, or in subtle nudges, it's all guidance. And it's all yours.

Consulting by Instinct
In those early projects, I was doing what came naturally: noticing gaps. Asking questions. Calling on my growing network. Making things work. I'd learned enough by then to spot misalignments from a mile away. Confusing menus, inefficient room layouts, undertrained staff, unexpressed brand values, missed opportunities in guest experience.

I didn't need to critique to feel smart. I didn't need

to be right. I wanted to help things flow like I'd been doing in other areas of my life.

I treated my new venture into wellness consulting like a form of healing. Because for me, it was.

It wasn't about fixing broken things. It was about creating alignment in well-being, between people and processes, between purpose and execution, between what a space promised and what it actually delivered.

And I realized something else along the way: my flow zone wasn't just in wellness delivery. It was in wellness architecture, the design of spaces, systems, and strategies that supported healing for everyone involved.

Power doesn't always roar. Sometimes it whispers. There's a quiet kind of strength in honoring your limits and redefining your work from the inside out.

The Patterns that Wellness Businesses Miss
As I stepped deeper into consulting, I started to notice recurring issues across wellness businesses, regardless of size, budget, or location.

Some were operational: broken systems, unclear

workflows, or staffing models that didn't make sense. Some were philosophical: a disconnect between the brand's messaging and what actually happened when a guest walked in. But the most common issue? Overcomplication.

Wellness doesn't have to be complicated. But somewhere along the way, many businesses started to believe it had to look a certain way to feel premium, layered protocols, multi-step experiences, fancy terminology that alienated rather than invited. And in that process, the soul of the offering got lost.

What frustrated me most wasn't the inefficiency, it was the missed opportunity. The potential for deep transformation was there, but it was buried beneath poor or non-existent training, aesthetic over-function, or leaders who were too burnt out to see clearly.

I realized that my soulful healing arts background had given me an edge: I knew how to hold space *and* how to streamline operations. I could expertly speak about chakras and cost-per-treatment. I could design intuitive floor plans and guide a team through energy-clearing experiences. I could speak the language of the practitioner, the guest, the GM, and C-Suite.

And that blend? I think it was rare. It was valuable. It worked.

What if your sensitivity was never a flaw, but a finely tuned compass? What if every part of your path, every beautiful moment you learned from was quietly preparing you to soar?

Leading from the Inside
All of this helped me develop what I now think of as my "Flow State", the place where natural talent, lived experience, and embodied wisdom all converge. It's where I make my best decisions. It's where I stop trying to prove myself and simply offer what I know.

I didn't set out to build a personal brand. I set out to build a life of service that made sense for my soul. And every time I chose alignment over approval, trust over perfection, embodiment over performance, I got closer to the version of myself I was always becoming.

Because that's the real business of being well. It's not just about wellness as a service. It's about wellness as a way of being. It's about creating what you need first, then letting it ripple outward.

Living the Truth Before Selling the Solution
I didn't start consulting because I had it all figured out. I started because I cared, and because I was willing to live my own medicine before offering it to anyone else.

That meant being well before preaching wellness. It meant pausing when I was depleted, saying no to clients who didn't align, raising my rates when the energy wasn't right, and walking away from projects that drained my creativity. It meant letting my nervous system lead instead of my ego.

It also meant narrowing my focus. In the beginning, I offered too much, said yes too often, and tried to be everything to everyone. But over time, I learned to specialize. I began to clearly understand my zone of impact: visionary hospitality, intuitive operations, and brand experiences that feel as good as they look.

That clarity didn't come from a marketing workshop. It came from living it.

When I finally embraced that being myself, fully and authentically, was the brand, everything shifted. I didn't have to chase opportunities. They found me. Because energy, when aligned, becomes magnetic.

And from that magnetism, my work grew. So did my peace.

On Becoming the Next Version of Yourself
Here's what I want you to remember:

• You don't have to wait until you feel ready. Embody who you want to become now.

• Strategy and soul are not opposites. They are partners. Let your intuition inform your planning.

• The business of being well starts with you. And the best way to lead is to live your message.

Ask yourself:

• What patterns am I here to interrupt?

• What comes easily to me that others find challenging?

• Where do I feel most in alignment, and how can I build from there?

You don't need to prove your worth to anyone, because you are already ready just as you are. The biggest step is simply to start.

Your life is your case study. Your presence is your resume.

If you've ever held space for others, take a moment now to hold space for yourself. What has your body taught you this season? What business instincts have been quietly waiting for your permission to lead with more softness, not less strategy?

_____
_____
_____
_____
_____
_____
_____
_____
_____
_____
_____
_____
_____
_____
_____
_____
_____

5

When the Body Speaks

"Healing isn't a detour...it's the foundation for every good thing I've built."

I didn't pivot gracefully. I stalled. I spiraled. I sat in the bath until the water went cold and still had no clarity. There wasn't some elegant resolution or a breakthrough breath. There was just a moment where I decided to stop forcing it. That moment didn't feel brave. It felt like giving up. But it wasn't. It was the beginning of a new kind of listening.

Some transformations don't happen in a flash of light—they arrive slowly, with the quiet insistence of pain that won't go away. For me, that pain was literal. My thirties were shaped by a decade-long struggle with PCOS, uterine fibroids, anemia, and chronic inflammation that left me exhausted, depleted, and constantly rearranging my life to accommodate symptoms I couldn't seem to heal away.

I had always thought of myself as someone who could handle pain. I was strong. Resilient. Capable. But at some point, even the most durable foundations crack. And what I began to realize—slowly, stubbornly, is that some of my capacity for suffering wasn't strength at all. It was conditioning. A deep-seated belief that pain was just part of being a woman, a mother, a healer. That belief, it turns out, is a lie.

Throughout those years, I adapted to living and working through discomfort. I kept going because I had to, but also because I loved what I was doing. I loved the people I served, the beauty I was building, the tiny glimmers of ease and magic that still found me between the harder moments. I loved my family and found immense joy in our everyday rituals, even when I was running on fumes. Kaya and I were building a life that looked, from the outside, vibrant and full. And in many ways, it was. But behind the scenes, because of my fibroids, I was bleeding heavily for three and a half weeks out of every month. I was managing meetings and motherhood with heating pads and Advil. I was burning out, not just from work, but from the quiet labor of enduring.

And yet there was always movement. In my own messy, often winding way, I kept evolving.

During those years, I used the forced times of rest to widen my lens of healing for work. I started leaning even more on my intuitive gifts, reading bodies, energy, spaces and places, especially as I moved further into the business side of wellness. I began consulting more frequently, not just offering services but offering strategy. My superpower was becoming clearer: I could walk into a space, observe everything: the flow, the staff dynamic, the energetic atmosphere, and know exactly where things needed to shift.

My body and energy reading skills translated surprisingly well into consulting. On hotel site visits, I'd sit in leadership meetings, take the tour, listen to the goals and pain points, and then quietly note what wasn't being said. The "medicine" at the end of each long day? A solo walk, no matter where I was. That was always where the answers revealed themselves. It wasn't just about decompressing, it was part of my process. I'd move my body, breathe, and reconnect with the land, letting the rhythm of my footsteps loosen the knots in my mind. The most beautiful ideas often arrived when I stopped trying to force them.

That's the thing about a place, it speaks. Especially in the world of wellness. Whether I was helping open a new spa or reimagine an existing one, I always started with the foundational questions: Who is this for? What is it trying to say? Where does it belong in the community? When will it thrive? And, most importantly, why does it matter? That old-school journalism framework I learned in college, who, what, when, where, why, never left me. It simply evolved into a process of helping brands find their voice, their meaning, their soul.

And once I knew that, once we had the essence, we could ask the next big question: What now?

A Deepening

These years weren't just about business growth, they were about internal excavation. Kaya and I decided to move our family back up to the Pacific

Northwest, to Bend, Oregon, and it gave me some needed space. Literal space, spiritual space, emotional space. And with that came a reckoning. I joined a long-term women's mastermind group focused on personal growth and financial expansion. It was less about strategy and more about deep listening, about being witnessed. These women became soul sisters, mirrors, and midwives for the version of me that was being born.

During that season, I found myself asking bigger questions. Not just about what I wanted to create, but about who I was when I wasn't creating anything at all. I was digging into old wounds, sifting through patterns and stories I'd inherited or adopted, and asking, "Do I still want to carry this?" It felt like a soul recomposition. My dreams became richer, more insistent. Like they were when I was young. Sometimes they were escape portals to other dimensions, sometimes they were sharp with warning. They were always full of symbols and clues.

I became curious, obsessed even, with how the women before me had navigated their lives. My grandmothers. My great-grandmother Ida, whose photographs I had found, laughing, surrounded by loved ones, pride and joy written across her face. She looked so happy. So full. I thought of Grandma Lillian often too, of how she quietly instilled wisdom through her daily rituals, walking, eating simply, living frugally but fully. The way she lived was a masterclass in wellness long before wellness became an industry.

During that time, I still loved my body, even when it betrayed me. Even when I was in intense pain. I moved it. I breathed. Nourished it as best I could. Let it rest when it was needed. I walked the dogs, Dio, who had been with us since our early San Diego days, and Lily, the Aussie mix I dreamed of before I found her in Bend. They became my co-regulators, my companions. Twice a day, we ventured out for walks and hikes, and with every step I felt a little more connected to myself, a little more grounded in who I was becoming.

Of course, none of this happened in isolation. Kaya was there through it all, supportive, steady, saying yes even when it meant rearranging his own life so I could pursue mine. He's the kind of partner who cheers for every version of me, who believes in my ideas before I've fully voiced them. And the kids, growing, thriving, reminding me daily of what really matters. Our life wasn't always smooth, but it was rich. Real. Full of joy, chaos, and grace.

My Dad and stepmom Katie also stayed close to us, as they lived nearby our new Oregon home. Present, loving, grounded in their own way. I often thought of how different that relationship felt compared to the slowly widening gap between my mom and me. That distance, decades in the making, wasn't dramatic, but it was real. The kind of drift that happens not through conflict, but through unmet expectations and emotional mismatches. It hurt. And I've grieved it in quiet ways. But it also clarified what I needed to feel safe and seen in adulthood.

Through it all, my closest friends stayed close. Even when I didn't have the bandwidth to reach out, they didn't let me disappear. They kept showing up, not with demands, but with presence. It reminded me that community doesn't always look like weekly catch-ups and long texts. Sometimes it's a simple "I'm here when you're ready," and the deep knowing that you are still loved, even in your silence.

The thing about chronic pain is that it's unseen. Most people in my life had no idea how much I was suffering. On the outside, I kept my vibe high. I always showed up as my best self, a grounded and calm presence, with care over my appearance and impact on my community. I still believed in leading by example, even when I wanted to collapse into the comfort of Kaya's arms and enter an exhausted deep sleep.

This chapter of life was a sojourn, a deep dive into the layered, dark places of who I am. And while it didn't always look productive or high impact, something important was happening under the surface. I was rapidly maturing emotionally. Leaning into my secret inner world in ways I hadn't expected. Getting clearer on what really matters. And after all the introspection, the deep work, the peeling back of layers, I felt it.

A knowing.

It was time to *let go*.

Not of my ambition or creativity or drive, but of the need to constantly prove, digest, or explain myself. I had crossed some invisible threshold. I no longer needed external permission to become the next version of myself. I gave it to myself.

Permission to Heal
The physical pain lingered loudly. I had tried everything from nutrition to herbs, rest, movement, acupuncture, yoga, more rest. I had invested in every angle of healing I knew for over ten years at this

point, but nothing could touch the relentless cycle I was in. Three and a half weeks of bleeding every month. Fatigue that layered over my bones like wet wool. Anemia that left me breathless from a simple grocery run. My body had given me everything it could. It was time I returned the favor.

A hysterectomy was never something I had considered. Frankly, the idea felt too dramatic. Too final. Too clinical. But sometimes, the body speaks so loudly that you can't ignore it anymore. I had an OB-GYN doctor who felt like a divine match. She was grounded, clear, and incredibly supportive. I was in her office discussing yet another alternative route. But her response made it simple: "You've done your time. You've tried it all. And now you get to be done. Have you ever considered getting a hysterectomy?"

And that was it. A deep exhale. A full stop. No, I had never considered that because I was too young, and it seemed like a big move when I had already been handling my symptoms for so long. But the way she spoke to me with respect, intellect, and realism clicked.

I kept my ovaries, which felt like an important choice. I still wanted the hormonal intelligence they offered. But removing the source of so much pain, so much unrelenting friction, felt like reclaiming space I didn't even know I had lost. And as wry as it sounds, the whole experience was oddly freeing. Major surgery, yes. But also? Major reset.

Like Marie Kondo-ing your uterus.

Letting go isn't always dramatic. Sometimes it just is. A door gently closing. A body finally exhaling. And a soft, steady voice inside saying: *you did the right thing.*

And just like that, I began to recover. Slowly at first. Then with more vitality than I'd had in years. I started Hormone Replacement Therapy, even though I still had the power of my ovaries, which helped tremendously, and found myself laughing more easily, working more joyfully, resting more intentionally. I could finally feel my full self returning, not the self I used to be, but someone new. Someone whole.

That decade of intense chronic symptoms taught me more than any leadership seminar or spiritual retreat ever could. It taught me how to listen. How to soften without collapsing. How to move through hard things without letting them harden me. Because in reality, things really had been hard for a long time. I became both stronger and more tender. Less performative, more peaceful.

And maybe that's the point of this chapter, and why I'm sharing it. Because I know I'm not the only one who's quietly endured seasons of pain while trying to build a beautiful life. I know what it's like to keep showing up, keep leading, keep caring for everyone else while your own system is burning down behind the scenes. And I also know this: it doesn't have to be like that forever.

There are seasons when the world expects us to perform wellness while quietly surviving it. Sometimes resilience looks like still showing up. Sometimes, it's just knowing when to stop pretending it doesn't hurt.

Sometimes healing doesn't come in the form of a perfect plan. Sometimes, it comes in the form of permission. To rest. To stop. To say, "This is enough."

And when you do, when you choose yourself fully, the world doesn't fall apart.

It opens up.

Where does your body feel like home—and where does it still feel like negotiation? What would it look like to create wellness not from a place of fixing, but of reverence?

6

The Repatterning

The Cost of Expansion: Choosing Growth Without Burnout

"The work gets better when you stop proving and start remembering who you are."

This was the integration I had been working toward. Not just building a business or a brand, but creating a rhythm that allowed me to be well and do well in real time.

One morning I opened my laptop and stared at a blank calendar block. It used to hold three back-to-back calls. I'd canceled them the week before, claiming that time for something I didn't even know I needed yet. Old me would have filled it with hustle, or guilt, maybe both.

But that day, I paused. I made tea. Sat in the sun for thirteen minutes. Just watched the light move across the floor. Nothing dramatic happened. But something real did. It was the first time in a long time my nervous system believed me. Trusted me to rest. Trusted me to choose differently.

It took time to build a rhythm that truly belonged to me. But eventually, I started designing my days on my own terms.

It's strange how a new city can become the backdrop to your becoming. For me, that city was San Antonio. The move wasn't a strategic pivot or a passion project—it was a necessity. A quiet knowing in my body, one that had learned to whisper instead of shout: it's time.

We had spent five years in beautiful Bend, Oregon. It had healed me in the ways I most needed at the time, through stillness, nature, and the softness of agreeing to a major surgery that would help me heal. But by the time my kids were old enough to navigate school without us hovering nearby, and the fog of nearly constant physical pain and inflammation had finally lifted, I found myself pacing again. Not the way I had in my twenties, desperate for the next big opportunity, but in a more grounded, internal way. It was like I could feel my purpose growing inside my body again, stretching out. I needed space.

San Antonio was never on any vision board. But the decision to move wasn't about the city, it was about who I could become there. I wanted less hustle, more flow. Less metaphorical frostbite, more sun. Less proving, more creating. The woman I had once been—visionary, determined, a little overcommitted to her work—was still in there, but now she was now a fully fledged, mature adult-me. I wanted my work to match the woman I was becoming.

And I didn't want to be tired anymore.

The fatigue I'm talking about isn't the kind you solve with green juice or a 90-minute nap. Yes, my health has been a contributing factor over the years. But with my newfound energy and sense of purpose, I wanted to develop cleaner boundaries.

It was the accumulation of a thousand small misalignments: working with clients who don't respect your time, entertaining conversations that drain instead of energize, doing favors for people who wouldn't lift a finger for you. For years, I had been collecting that kind of fatigue like a hidden tax and thinking I was becoming stronger for it. It wasn't until we landed in South Texas that I finally decided I was done paying it.

At first, I tried to go slower. I filled my calendar with gentler things—long walks with Kaya, midday meditation breaks, teaching a few yoga classes each week, and lunches under the sun with my laptop closed. But even in my rest, there was an undercurrent of desire. I didn't want to stop growing—I just wasn't interested in a lack of clarity any longer. I wanted to build something real and sustainable without losing myself in the process. I had seen too many women I admired burn up in pursuit of their own brilliance.

I wasn't going to be one of them.

In the quiet hours of those first few months in San Antonio, I started to reset—but differently. I asked myself more questions than I answered. I stopped trying to fix things that didn't want to be fixed. I started taking the emotional temperature of the rooms I entered, and if the vibe was cold or condescending, I left.

It was also around this time that I began to understand energy in an entirely new way. I had always been sensitive and intuitive, but I had never given much structure to it. My decisions had often been based on a mix of logic, instinct, and spiritual nudges. But one afternoon, while browsing through an old note archive, I stumbled upon my Human Design chart. I hadn't really connected to this method of self discovery a few years earlier when a friend gave it to me. But now, something clicked. Curiosity turned into deep interest and application.

For years, I had identified with being a Manifestor— someone who initiates, who leads. It made sense based on how others saw me. But when reviewing my chart, I learned I was a Generator. A responder. A cultivator. Someone meant to wait for things to spark before acting.

I cried.

Not because it changed everything—but because it explained everything. The burnouts. The overextensions. The deep, bone-level tiredness that would sneak in after I pushed too hard for too long. I had been trying to live like someone I wasn't. Now I know why it never felt sustainable.

Meeting Myself Again

This discovery wasn't just a fun fact. It reshaped how I showed up in my work, my home, my relationships. I stopped saying yes to things that didn't light me up. I tested out taking a pause before committing to things, even if they seemed exciting. I started paying attention to my body's signals—not as inconveniences, but as sacred data.

The clients I took on during this time started to feel different too. Because I wasn't exclusively chasing high-ticket contracts or trying to land splashy name brands, I was able to lean more into my network and what had become a solid reputation. I wanted soul alignment and clarity. I wanted to work with people who weren't afraid to ask hard questions and who valued the how as much as the what, like I did.

One of the most healing things I did during this period, alongside tidying up my business boundaries, was allow myself to be loved in a new way.

Kaya and I had always had a solid relationship, but like many couples, we had weathered seasons where things felt lopsided. For years, I felt like I had been the one holding it all. Logistics. Planning. Emotional labor. The invisible work of family management. It wasn't that he didn't want to help; it's that I hadn't known how to let go.

Texas helped me let go.

There's something about starting over that makes it easier to renegotiate old roles. With no familiar rhythms to fall back on, we had to make new ones. And in that fresh space, I began to soften. I stopped performing productivity and started practicing presence. Kaya noticed. He stepped up. We began having more open conversations about emotional labor and energy equity. Slowly, the balance began to shift.

And if I'm honest, the balance now tilts in my favor. He's been more than generous with holding space for my healing, growth, and dreams.

We laugh about it sometimes—how long I carried so much and how naturally he's picked up the slack. But instead of guilt, what I feel is readiness. I'm preparing to step back in again. Not into the over-functioning version of myself, but into my next chapter of softness. The one where I create from overflow, instead of following the old patterns of depletion when things get hard.

One of the trickiest parts of growth is that it often masquerades as destruction. Something must fall away to make space. And in those early Texas years, the thing I had to let go of most was my old definition of success.

Ten years earlier, I would have told you success looked like a full schedule, nonstop travel, glowing testimonials, and being seen as a go-to in my field. I wanted to be undeniable. Unshakeable. Known.

But here's the thing: *being known is only satisfying when you're being seen for who you actually are.* And somewhere along the way, I had become a version of myself that was far too palatable. Too packaged. Too "perfect" for people who, in truth, never even paid attention. For the most part, everyone else is mostly focused on simply moving through their own lives to worry about what others are doing. I hadn't been performing in a way that was fake, but I had been editing myself to stay safe.

I had to ask: What would success look like if I didn't care who was watching?

There is nothing passive about softness. It's a strength that knows when to listen, when to rest, when to stay. It's what happens when you stop performing strength and start embodying truth.

The answer came softly, in moments.

Success was waking up without dread. Moving through my day without rushing. Feeling proud of my work even if no one else applauded. Making money in a way that didn't make me question my ethics or ignore my body's signals. Creating impact without sacrificing intimacy, health, or sanity.

Success became internal.

What If...?
I began playing a mental game I now return to often. I call it What if...? But instead of asking from fear, *I flipped it into possibility.*

What if this idea is the one that changes everything?

What if the right collaborator is already watching?

What if saying no to this opportunity creates the exact space I need for a better one to arrive?

It wasn't about toxic positivity. It was about giving myself permission to expect miracles.

This inner game helped me rewire the narrative that ambition had to come with anxiety. I stopped defaulting to stress and started choosing strategy. And when I caught myself slipping into old patterns of proving or overworking, I didn't shame myself—I paused. I got curious. I asked what I needed.

Sometimes it was a snack.

Sometimes it was a break.

Sometimes it was a phone call with a trusted friend who reminded me that I am not my output.

It's powerful when the voice inside you becomes louder than the noise around you. When alignment feels like direction. When self-trust starts to feel like home.

Lessons in Balance – From Perfectionism to Real Fulfillment

I used to believe balance was something I could achieve if I only scheduled my life precisely enough—if I worked longer hours, said yes to more opportunities, and orchestrated every detail to perfection. Then I realized that perfection is a moving target. It doesn't matter how many hours you put in or how meticulously you plan; if your goal is to be without flaws, you'll never feel satisfied.

For a while, I had let perfectionism run my life. Have you ever typed and retyped an email, anxious over a single phrase that might be misread? Or triple-checked your calendar to squeeze in just one more meeting, believing it would make all the difference? That was me, obsessing over details like font choices in a presentation or the exact shade of spa linens a client should use.

Spoiler alert: The more I chased perfection, the further balance slipped from my grasp. My health—physically and emotionally—paid the price. I worked late into the night, skipping meals, skipping rest, and basically skipping life. I'd collapse into bed feeling empty, even though my project list was meticulously checked off.

Eventually, I had to face the truth: I was missing the point of the very wellness philosophy I was supposed to be championing. How could I advocate for rest, self-care, and holistic well-being if I was burning the candle at both ends? This realization hit me like a 100 foot wave. Wellness wasn't just something I did for others; it was something I had to embody for myself.

Five Common Mistakes I Made in the Pursuit of Perfection

1. Over-Scheduling in the Name of Productivity
For a long time, I equated a jam-packed schedule with success. It took hitting a near-breaking point to recognize that space—unscheduled time—is essential for creativity and sanity.

2. Believing That More Hours = More Impact
I poured entire days into tasks that could have been done more effectively—and often more creatively—if I had taken strategic breaks.

3. Trying to Please Everyone
In an effort to be helpful, I said yes to every project, every phone call, every new inquiry. Eventually, I realized I was stretched too thin to do anything well.

4. Expecting a Linear Path to Success
Life rarely unfolds in a neat upward trajectory. I had to learn to pivot, adapt, and be okay with the reality that progress sometimes comes in waves and curves.

5. Treating Self-Care as a Reward Instead of a

Requirement

I used to see rest as something I'd "earned" after completing enough work. But the truth is, rest is a fuel source, not an optional bonus.

Tools That Shifted My Perspective

Energy Tracking: Instead of just counting hours, I tracked how each task made me feel. Did client calls energize me or drain me? Did I leave enough buffer to process new ideas? Over time, I recalibrated my schedule to maximize tasks that sustained my energy and minimized those that didn't.

The 'Good Enough' Rule: Once I reached a point where a proposal or document was solid, I stopped nitpicking. Good enough truly is enough, because in the real world, feedback and iteration can refine any rough edges.

By loosening my grip on perfection, I discovered something profound: I was more present, more joyful, and, ironically, more *productive* because I wasn't stuck in an endless cycle of self-critique.

Refinement

I also began playing with boundaries in a whole new way. Not just the kind that protects your time, but the kind that protects your frequency.

I stopped picking up calls from people who always led with drama. I muted conversations that drained me. I kindly said no to coffee dates that felt like disguised "pick-your-brain" sessions. And maybe most importantly, I stopped trying to rescue anyone who didn't ask for help. My professional circle, while always expanding, started to become more refined at the same time.

For years, I had built my business—and parts of my identity—on being the one who could fix it, hold it, plan it, lead it. But being good at something doesn't mean you have to do it forever. I didn't want to be the savior. I wanted to be The Strategist. The Visionary. The Mentor who calls people forward, not the fixer who mops up their mess. There's a difference.

When you finally stop over-functioning for others, it gets quieter. Sometimes painfully so. People fall away. Invitations slow down. You wonder if you're being selfish or cold. But what you're really doing is recalibrating. And if you stay with it long enough, the right people find their way to your doorstep. And when they do, it's not loud. It's aligned. And you're in the right headspace to pay attention and receive.

During this chapter of life, I also began to take more creative risks. I wasn't just offering services—I was now building frameworks. Original IP. Big ideas that required courage and conviction. I began structuring my work around the energy of fewer meetings, deeper connections, and better outcomes.

Fewer clients.

Deeper partnerships.

Better boundaries.

It sounds simple, but it's revolutionary when you've spent most of your career trying to scale by doing more.

I stopped chasing the fantasy that I needed to be booked solid to feel worthy. Instead, I asked: What would it look like to be paid well to be myself? Not just the polished, curated, consultant version—but the honest, complex, good-humored person being I actually am?

This question unlocked everything. I went through cycles of refining my offers. Of educating myself further in my areas of specialization and interest. Letting go of anything that no longer felt alive. I created containers where I could bring my full self—strategy, spirituality, business acumen, creative direction, and intuition—all in one place. And people started responding. Not because I had the loudest message, but because it was real.

There's a resonance that comes when you're no longer pretending. And once you feel it, you can't go back.

Strategy doesn't mean losing your soul. You can build with vision and heart. With clarity and curiosity. With spreadsheets and sage. You don't have to choose.

There was also a consistent, buzzing joy in this season. Joy that felt rightfully earned. Joy I didn't feel the need to post or explain. Walks through gardens and landscapes of the places I visited. Shared meals full of inspiration and passionately cultivated concepts. Late-night business ideas that turned into viable programs. Deep, satisfying conversations with Kaya over a simple home cooked meal and a glass of wine.

This was what I had wanted all along. Not only outward success. Not just impact. But *life*. The kind of life where I could be with my family instead of recovering from work. The kind of life where I could write freely, create boldly, and advise from a place of fullness and gratitude. The kind of life where I didn't need to shrink myself to fit someone else's definition of success and professionalism. I was building that life.

And while the path wasn't always clear or easy, I had one thing I had never had in such abundance before: self-trust.

This is where the work begins to stretch beyond you. Where your story becomes a blueprint, your voice becomes an invitation, and your presence becomes a map for others to follow.

Trust is the Answer
By the time I hit my early forties, the internal terrain had shifted.

I was no longer trying to prove I belonged in the room. I *knew* I belonged, and had brought along great people with me. Not because of titles or client rosters or what I charged, but because I had earned my way into every seat I held, and not one of them had ever been handed to me. For years, I had walked into boardrooms, hotel suites, strategy sessions, and spa back offices quietly tracking the energy, mapping the needs, observing the gaps no one else seemed to notice.

Now, I had the vocabulary, and the confidence, to name it. I had built my own "board room", and had cultivated a team of elite players around me.

The clarity that had begun in Bend, and sharpened in San Antonio, and had crystallized into something new and exciting. Something bigger than any one offer or client engagement. It was a way of working. A lens. A strategic approach that could support wellness businesses beyond surface-level aesthetics or basic development. I wanted to help them expand in a way that felt both true and future-focused—starting at the soul level.

So I built a model around that. A clean, intuitive, no-fluff way of moving brands forward without draining their team, compromising their integrity, or confusing their audience. I didn't want to offer one-off project services anymore, I wanted to guide transformation. And that required a clear, phased process.

The first phase focused on clarity and evolution. Not a bloated audit or a jargon-heavy slide deck, but a focused conversation around who the brand was becoming. We'd get clear on the friction points, the values, the deeper story, and the gap between intention and execution. We'd strip away what no longer fit. This part was often deeply emotional, because let's be honest, most business problems are personal problems in disguise.

Then came phase two: strategy and momentum. Once the business had realigned with itself, we could begin the work of scaling, innovating, repositioning, or refreshing. Sometimes that looked like rebuilding operational systems. Sometimes it meant launching a new vertical or experience. Sometimes it meant rewriting the entire narrative, from pitch deck to programming.

But always, it meant breathing life back into the business.

And I didn't do it alone.

By this point, I had cultivated a tight circle of high-level collaborators. Brilliant minds and warm hearts who shared my values and matched my standards. These weren't just people I brought in for the occasional project. They were creative thinkers, tacticians, artists, strategists, brand architects, writers, and advisors I deeply trusted. People I would bring into the room with zero hesitation. People who could hold nuance, deliver excellence, and bring out the best in every idea.

Together, we became a kind of quiet powerhouse.

We didn't need fanfare. We needed trust, clarity, and momentum—and we delivered it. Not through one-size-fits-all frameworks, but through custom, soulful strategy. No smoke and mirrors. No templated gloss. Just the real stuff, delivered by real people, with real results.

I finally felt like I had built something worthy of the years I had put in. Something that mirrored my lived experience and allowed me to show up fully— visionary, intuitive, strategic, deeply human.

This was my next level. And I didn't have to shout to be heard.

And here's the part I didn't expect: I loved it.

I loved leading without rescuing. I loved guiding without controlling. I loved being the calm, clear voice in rooms that were often overwhelmed or overthinking. I loved showing people that vision and structure didn't have to live on opposite ends of a spectrum—they could hold hands.

For so long, I'd held the identity of "consultant" as something noble but exhausting. It implied hours, availability, and constant delivery. But the way I work now is different. It's centered, customized, and collaborative. It's about holding a higher standard. Creating outcomes, not just deliverables. Being deeply embedded in a brand's evolution, but only where it makes sense. A true partner—not a fixer, not a cog in the machine.

It also gave me more space to be.

I started writing again. Longer pieces. Thought leadership. Creative strategy memos. Some days I worked from beautiful hotels, others from my sunlit kitchen table with Lily curled up beside me. I didn't need a Pinterest-perfect workspace—I needed resonance. I needed to feel proud of what I was doing, how I was doing it, and who I was doing it with.

And finally, I did.

Stepping into this evolution also required me to upgrade how I related to time.

I used to equate being busy with being important. I

wore full calendars like badges of honor, secretly believing that if I wasn't a little overwhelmed, I probably wasn't doing enough. But now, I saw time differently. I saw it as something sacred and strategic.

Time was where my energy got translated into outcomes.

So I *finally* stopped glorifying the hustle. I created blocks in my week that were truly off-limits. No client calls, no catch-up meetings, no social scrolling. Just vision time. Integration time. Reflection time. That was where the real magic happened.

There's something sacred about living in rhythm instead of reaction. When your life starts to match your values, and your calendar reflects your actual heart, you know you've come home to something real. Because truthfully? The more space I gave myself, the more potent my work became.

This was the opposite of burnout. This was expansion without depletion.

I wasn't "balancing" anything anymore. I was choosing, intentionally, what got my energy. And anything that didn't feel like a "hell yes" was a clear *no.*

An Expansion

There's a moment in every woman's life, if she's lucky, when she stops shrinking to fit other people's expectations and starts expanding into her own.

This was mine.

I had learned to lead differently. My work no longer revolved around proving I was the most prepared person in the room. I wasn't trying to impress anyone anymore, I was simply telling the truth. Asking the right questions. Following the threads that led to alignment, innovation, and momentum. People listened because the clarity was contagious.

I wasn't doing it alone, either.

My collaborators, each of them brilliant in their own right, have been instrumental. These are the people I call when a project needs more depth, a different vision, or a specialized execution. They aren't yes-people. They aren't over-hyped generalists. They're the kind of professionals who hold their own in any room and elevate the work simply by being in it.

Together, we've created magic. Quietly, strategically, consistently.

The best collaborations don't ask you to shrink. They expand you. They remind you that you're not meant to carry the whole vision alone, and that brilliance grows in shared space.

Every project we took on became a co-creation: rooted in integrity, delivered with excellence, and infused with care. Because that's the thing. Care is the most underrated part of successful business. It's not just about metrics and milestones. It's about how you treat people. How you hold vision. How you honor energy.

I had no interest in building a brand that moved fast but felt soulless. I wanted to build something that meant something. With this team, I could.

The Flow Zone
I began to notice how often people used the phrase "next level" without actually knowing what it meant for them.

For me, the next level wasn't louder, it was quieter. It wasn't bigger, it was sharper. It wasn't about adding more, it was about refining what was already brilliant.

The next level meant working with leaders who were brave enough to pause, ask better questions, and redesign their entire approach if needed. Leaders who weren't just looking for answers but were open to becoming the kind of people who could hold better answers. My clients didn't just want growth, they wanted legacy. They wanted purpose baked into every part of the business.

And that? That's where I thrive. Because I don't just see what's working, I see what's possible.

I see where the friction is. I see where the misalignment hides. I see where potential is being capped by old systems or timid leadership or unclear communication. I see the gap between what a brand says it values and how it actually shows up. And then, I help close it.

Sometimes that looks like executive strategy. Sometimes it looks like emotional excavation. Sometimes it looks like creating bold new revenue models or scrapping old offers entirely. Sometimes it looks like flying across the country to walk a property in silence before saying a single word.

Because the soul of a business speaks, if you know how to listen.

This is the work I'm most proud of.

When your joy becomes watching others thrive, you know you're living in legacy. This is what leadership looks like: lifting as you climb, witnessing without rescuing, and celebrating without comparison.

It's work that asks me to be present, embodied, and awake. It's work that doesn't let me hide behind a title or a slide deck. It requires me to be both expert and student, teacher and translator, strategist and storyteller. It's work that stretches me into deeper layers of myself—and somehow, always leaves me more energized than when I began.

And it's sustainable. Not because it's easy, but because it's true.

I finally understood what it meant to live and lead from my Flow Zone; that sacred space where my deepest gifts and highest contributions meet. The place where I don't have to force anything. Where I feel divinely resourced. Where ideas come fast, and clarity feels like currency. Where my lived experience, my intuition, my strategy brain, and my weirdly specific spa nerd wisdom all get to play in the same sandbox. This is where the best results happen.

This is where the real legacy begins.

Discernment and Clarity
Midlife, for me, didn't come with a breakdown. It came with a reckoning. I wasn't chasing balance anymore. I had earned alignment. And I was willing to walk away from anything, or anyone, that tried to pull me out of it. I began to protect my peace like it was part of my job. Because it was.

Peace is where vision lands. Peace is where right relationships thrive. Peace is where I hear myself most clearly. And so, I built my business around it. Not at the expense of results—but in service of them.

Today, I do the kind of work that lights me up and lights up the people I work with. I help brands evolve, founders clarify, and teams align. I travel when it matters, write when I'm inspired, and rest without apology. I work with the smartest, most capable people I know. I trust my intuition as much as I trust the numbers. And I say no with love and zero guilt.

Because the cost of expansion, I've learned, doesn't have to be burnout. It can be boundaries, joy, and trust. It can be you, fully expressed, operating in flow.

And once you find that rhythm, there's no going back.

There was no single moment where everything clicked. But there was a shift. One day I walked into a hotel boardroom and didn't shrink. I offered my insights, mapped out solutions, and held the room. Not by force, but by clarity. That's when I knew I was no longer just participating. I was leading.

7

Arrival and Still Waters

Arrival and Still Waters
Leadership that lasts isn't built on hustle. It is built on clarity, rhythm, and the ability to self-resource through every season.
"Balance isn't something I found. It's something I built."

We're going together. If I can, we all can. The thing no one tells you about arriving is that it doesn't feel like fireworks. It feels like a steady hum. A rhythm you've earned. The quiet confidence of a woman who no longer rushes to prove herself or contort to fit a room.

It feels like slipping into your favorite soft pants after a long flight.

Like knowing which projects are worth your energy before the pitch deck is even done loading. Like turning down the noise, internally and externally, and realizing the power you were chasing was never out there at all. It was here. In your belly. In your breath. In your morning cup of tea.

After decades of defining success by external metrics like client wins, magazine features, project budgets, and packed schedules, I started asking a different question: Does this feel like alignment or performance?

I had the answers all along. I just wasn't listening to the right part of me. In this season of my life, I'm listening more than I ever have before. And I'm building everything from that still, centered place: my consulting work, my family rhythm, my health, my friendships, my future. The quiet water of my life is not boring. It's beautiful. It's rich. It's precise.

Stillness doesn't mean nothing is happening.

Stillness means I'm no longer betraying myself for motion.

Thrive Mode
With fond emotion, I recall the moment when I looked around and realized I was no longer in survival mode. Not in my work, my marriage, or my body. Not even in my thoughts.

The internal chaos that had once felt normal, the low-grade stress humming underneath everything... it was gone. I hadn't noticed the exact moment it left. But I noticed when peace arrived. And it was shocking how quiet it was. How unceremonious. How... simple.

It showed up in the form of slow mornings and creative ideas that didn't require a marketing sprint. It showed up in the way I could hear my children's laughter in the background and actually register it without being pulled under by guilt or hurry.

It showed up in the mirror. My face is softer, more

beautiful, my eyes steadier. This was the arrival. Not a single milestone or a contract signed, but the moment I felt proud of the life I'd built without trying to escape it or constantly improve it.

I'd lived long enough in the fire of becoming. Now, I was ready to live in the water of being.

What no one tells you about midlife is that it's not a crisis. It's a portal. And if you're brave enough to walk through it, without dragging all your old habits and noise and masks, you get something miraculous in return. You don't have to be finished to feel fulfilled. Arrival isn't a finish line, it's a deep breath. A quiet knowing. A moment when you realize… you're right where you're meant to be. And you have been all along.

You get *yourself* back. Not the version of yourself you had to create to get the job or hold the relationship or keep up appearances. Not the online version or the curated version or the hard-won, high-achieving version.

You get the core of you, and with that comes a clarity so sharp, it cuts through any of the old bullshit. You no longer entertain things out of obligation. You no longer say yes to be polite. You no longer care about being the smartest or most interesting person in the room—because the rooms you walk into now are curated by values, not ego.

This has been the deepest joy of arriving: the ability to co-create my days with such precision and devotion that even the hard ones feel anchored in purpose. That doesn't mean I don't experience doubt or pressure or heartbreak. I do. I just don't abandon myself in response to it anymore. I've learned to stay put instead of escaping. To trust that everything I've built so far can hold me, because I built it from a place of integrity. That includes my marriage. My parenting. My work. My team. My friendships. My hope. Each piece has been forged with intention. Even rest is intentional now.

We don't talk enough about how much practice it takes to learn how to rest. Especially for those of us who were praised for our drive, our perfectionism, our hyper-responsibility. *We were given applause for the very things that kept us disconnected from our bodies.*

Now, rest is a pillar. Not a reward. Not a treat. A pillar.

Some of my most important decisions are made in

the bathtub. Or during a nap. Or while walking with Kaya around the block with no phones, no agenda, no pressure to process anything out loud. Just steps. Just breath. Just belonging.

This is what I mean when I say I'm living from a place of still waters. It's not passive. It's powerful. Stillness is not stagnation. It's stewardship. My mission now isn't just consulting. It's legacy weaving. It's regenerative leadership. It's a model of what's possible when women stop shrinking, stop explaining, and start trusting the deeper rhythm underneath their ambition.

And I am stewarding the most aligned version of my life to date.

The evolution into this version of myself required letting go of everything that made me impressive but kept me disconnected. I had to unlearn urgency. I had to unhook from the addiction to being needed. I had to let softness come in and reshape me—not as a weakness, but as a superpower.

Now, my power lives in my nervous system. It is in my calendar, and in my posture. It facilitates recovery when I spiral, and reveals itself in how little I need to say to be heard.

People assume you reach this point by becoming more. More accomplished, more polished, more perfect. But that's not the truth. You reach this point by becoming less performative and more present. Less afraid. More aligned. Less fragmented. More whole.

There's a steadiness that comes from being fully known—not just by others, but by yourself. That steadiness has changed the way I create, the way I delegate, the way I move through the world. It's the difference between building for approval and building for legacy. And let me be clear: legacy is not about ego. Legacy is about imprint and the ripple effect of how you live, how you love, how you lead.

On Legacy
I used to think legacy was something you left behind, but now I understand it's something you live in real time. It's how you show up to hard conversations, or the energy you bring into a meeting. It's the kind of parent you are when no one's watching. It's how you treat people who can't offer you anything in return.

That's what people remember. That's what shapes the energy field around you. That's the ripple effect of a woman who's done her work.

These days, I feel no pressure to dominate the conversation. I'd rather ask a great question. One that unlocks something, or shifts the room into a more innovative space.

I've come to understand that the greatest mark of a leader isn't her credentials—it's her capacity. Her capacity to hold multiple complex truths at once. To hold tension without collapse. To hold power without posturing. To hold herself, even when the path forward isn't crystal clear. I hold more now, because I've finally learned how to be held by the world.

Held by grace, and by the rhythms that nourish me. By the structures I've carefully designed to support—not suppress—my creativity. I'm no longer afraid of that spaciousness. I don't panic when the calendar isn't packed. I don't mistake stillness for stagnation. Stillness is now where I hear the next right step. Stillness is where I reconnect with the future.

In fact, my best ideas no longer come from whiteboarding or brainstorming. They come from long walks. From meditation. From swimming. From standing in beautiful spaces with my palms open to the sun. From laughing with my family around the dinner table. From opening my heart to joy in the most ordinary places. That's where the magic lives now. In the mundaneness of a well-designed life.

I've spent the last few years designing not just business models, but entire ways of being. Systems that protect wellness instead of extract from it. Calendars that reflect actual capacity instead of fantasy-level productivity. Offers that feel regenerative to deliver, not just profitable to sell. That kind of design takes a different lens. It's not just about optimization. It's about orientation. Orientation toward wholeness. Toward truth. Toward freedom.

A Settling
At this stage, I'm not interested in proving I can do it all myself.

I've already done it all myself. I know what that feels like. And I know how it burns you up from the inside.

What excites me now is co-creation—with people who have vision, skill, integrity, and the kind of self-awareness that makes collaboration feel like play, not politics. My team isn't just talented—they're thoughtful. Clear. Kind. Sharp. They're experts in their own right, and I trust them with my clients because I trust them with my name.

I'd spent too many years trying to explain or defend or dumb down my ideas in rooms that weren't built to hold a woman like me. Now, I build the rooms, and decide who's in them. I decide how we communicate. I set the tone with both strength and softness.

Because here's the thing: excellence doesn't have to feel rigid. Excellence can feel like a flow state. It can feel creative, lush, and intuitive. It can feel like laughing mid-meeting, crying mid-milestone, and taking a full-body breath when something lands. The spaces I lead now feel like that.

And the women I work with—the ones who've also built something from scratch, who've weathered storms and raised babies and buried dreams and come back stronger—they feel it, too. There's a knowing between us. A shorthand. A shared language.

We're not here to hustle for crumbs. We're here to redefine the table entirely, and we're doing it with intention. With levity. With bold boundaries and healed nervous systems and better questions. I'm still ambitious. But my ambition doesn't roar the way it used to.

Now, it hums, it whispers, and it sings.

I want to leave every space I enter a little brighter, a little clearer, a little more alive. Whether it's a boardroom or a hotel spa or my kitchen table, I want people to feel something when they're with me. Not because I'm trying to impress them, but because I'm grounded enough to be with them. Fully. Freely. Without a mask.

That's the beauty of this chapter: I'm not afraid of being seen anymore. In fact, I've built a life where I want to be seen. In my softness, leadership, love, and in my full, sacred humanity.

And the people I've drawn close to—my clients, my friends, my children, Kaya—see me more clearly than I've ever allowed before.

Because I'm not hiding anymore.

A Nurturing of Self
Motherhood has shifted, too.

The physical intensity has faded, but the emotional clarity is sharper than ever. My kids are growing into themselves—independent, creative, funny, and beautifully distinct—and I'm growing right alongside them.

There was a time when I measured my mothering by output: the weekly dinner menu, schedules managed, meltdowns averted, all of us getting from point A to B intact. Now, I measure it by presence. By connection. By the way they still come to me—not for answers, but for grounding.

I try to meet them where they are, without over-functioning, without rescuing, without turning their growth into my project. That shift has taken work. It has required me to let go of control, to stop over-identifying with their experiences, and to allow more space for their choices, for my peace, for all of us to be human.

It's the same lesson I've brought into my marriage.

Kaya and I have been through every season: love, struggle, reinvention, exhaustion, re-commitment. But what's different now is that we no longer default to performance or roles. We talk about the emotional labor split. We laugh more. We stretch. We repair quickly. And we've made softness a core value. Not just in our tone, but in how we approach our time, our goals, our shared energy. He holds so much with me and for me. And I've finally allowed myself to soften into that. Not as a weakness, but as a choice. As a powerful reclamation of trust and rest and shared momentum.

There is a stillness in our home that doesn't come from silence—it comes from deep respect. From rhythm. From the kind of alignment that's been built, tested, and chosen again and again. And here's the part that still surprises me: I'm not bored. I thought stillness might feel like boredom. I thought ease might mean I'd lose my edge. I thought peace might turn me into someone dull.

But the truth? I've never felt more alive.

The joy is sharper. The intimacy is keener. The ideas come faster. The friendships are deeper. The decisions are cleaner. My body feels stronger. My days feel sacred. Even when they're messy, and even when they're hard. *Especially* when they're ordinary. Because the ordinary has become a gift again. Not something to escape. Not a stepping stone. Not a performance.

Just life. Fully lived. Fully loved.

A Circle

I used to think that one day, I'd *arrive* at a version of myself that was done. Fully healed. Fully balanced. Fully certain. But I know better now. There is no finish line, there is only deeper integration, alignment, and truth.

What's changed is my capacity to walk forward without fear. To sit with uncertainty without collapsing. To move with grace even when the plan shifts—because it always does.

My life, this work, this rhythm… it's not static. It's alive. And so am I.

I still have goals. Big ones. I want my work to ripple across industries. I want the people I serve to feel powerful, safe and wildly seen. I want to shift the standard—not just in wellness, but in business, leadership and hospitality. I want the next generation of visionaries to know they don't have to sacrifice themselves to succeed.

But none of that can happen if I abandon the very truth I practice: that wellness isn't a reward for burnout. It's a baseline. It's a birthright. It's a blueprint for a different way of being. So I keep walking forward aligned in my mission to make a positive impact.

I'm walking through partnerships that excite me and ideas that light me up. I walk through family dinners and sunset walks and weekends off the grid. I walk through client retreats and keynote speeches and hotel site visits with my feet planted and my intuition on. I walk through it all with a soft strength that doesn't need to announce itself to be felt.

I walk with women who are doing the same—no longer fighting to be heard in rooms that weren't built for them, but creating new rooms, new systems, new standards. We're not just walking, we're widening the path.

And if you've read this far, maybe you're one of us, too.

Maybe you're someone who's been holding too much, giving too much, waiting for permission to soften, to reimagine, to arrive. This is your permission. Not to start over—but to start differently. From a place of wisdom. From a place of wholeness. From a place of deep, internal success that no one can take from you.

Because when you arrive in your own life—truly arrive—it's not just for you.

It's for all of us.

We're going together. If I can, we all can.

What does "arrival" look like in your life—not as an endpoint, but as a way of being? Describe a moment when you felt at peace with who you are, even if nothing external had changed.

Where in your life are you still performing instead of aligning? Be honest about the spaces, roles, or relationships where you feel the pull to prove, please, or produce.

How does your current relationship to rest reflect your values—or contradict them? What would it look like to let rest become a pillar, not a reward?

What parts of yourself are asking to be held more gently? Consider how softness could enhance your leadership, your relationships, or your daily rhythm.

If legacy is how you live, not what you leave behind—what energy are you weaving into the spaces you touch today? Think about your imprint at work, at home, and in moments no one sees. What do you want people to feel because you were there?

_____
_____
_____
_____
_____
_____
_____
_____
_____
_____
_____
_____
_____
_____
_____
_____
_____
_____
_____
_____

This simple framework has guided my own life, and I offer it to you as a way to move forward with clarity and rhythm.

Clarity: Know what's true for you—no noise, no guilt.

Rhythm: Move at the speed of your nervous system, not your notifications.

Presence: Let how you show up matter more than how you're perceived.

Power: Define success by your own metrics, and own your impact without apology.

These four elements are not linear. They spiral, cycle, and evolve. Use them as a compass to realign your energy, your decisions, and your leadership—whenever you feel pulled off center.

Here's what it looked like for me when each part of the Compass showed up:

Clarity: I rewrote my offerings to match who I am now. Not who I was five years ago.

Rhythm: I stopped doing Monday morning meetings. Took walks instead. Gave my week space to start soft.

Presence: At a retreat, I didn't talk. Others pitched.

I just listened. And it felt good.

Power: I raised my rates. Didn't pad the ask. Didn't flinch.

This is what it means to live it. Not with perfection. Just with choice.

You've just walked through my story. My becoming. My thresholds.

This next page isn't a conclusion. It's an offering. A way to return to yourself when the world pulls you too far out.

This isn't a framework. It's a frequency... and it's yours now.

Introducing:
The Be Well, Do Well Compass

A compass isn't a checklist. It's a returning. A way back to your own rhythm when the world tries to speed you up or pull you off course. Use this compass to support the building of your own field guide.

Clarity
   Not everyone's truth is your truth.
   You don't need more input. You need your own signal.

Clarity sounds like:
   "This decision fits me now."
   "That relationship served its season."
   "This 'yes' honors my whole body."

Rhythm
   You're not behind. You're not late.
   You're allowed to move at the pace of your own breath.

Rhythm feels like:
   Letting Monday start in silence.
   Building in margins, not back-to-backs.
   Choosing a slow walk over a scroll.

Presence

You are not what you produce.

Your presence is the offering.

Presence looks like:

Saying less and listening deeper.

Trusting the room will feel you without the pitch.

Letting the moment be what it is, not what it should be.

Power

This isn't loud. It isn't performative.

Power is knowing you no longer need permission.

Power moves like:

Raising your rates without apology.

Saying no and not spiraling.

Building your business around your nervous system, not someone else's timeline.

Use this Compass when you feel pulled out of yourself. When the calendar fills too fast. When the old patterns knock. When the future wants your presence, not just your plans. This isn't a framework. It's a frequency.

A woman recently told me she read an early version of this Compass and cried. Not because it was poetic.

Because it was plain. Because for the first time, someone had named the difference between pushing and power. She stopped auditioning. Stopped justifying. Walked into a meeting and simply said what she meant. And when I asked her what changed, she said this: 'You made it sound like it was already mine. I just had to claim it.'

The Be Well, Do Well Compass

I stopped surviving. I started shaping my days forward, with clarity and care. This chapter isn't just a reflection. It's a promise to live on purpose.

8

Living Well on My Own Terms

Living Well On My Own Terms
"When you trust your pace, the right path becomes undeniable."

The truth is, I still catch myself over explaining. I still want to be understood more than I want to be right, and I want to be loved. I still struggle with slowing down when everything's going right. I still question whether I'm too much or not enough, depending on the day. I've built a life that feels more true than ever. But none of it is perfect. None of it is neat. That's the part I want you to know: being well isn't about resolution. It's about returning. Again and again.

My dream begins with a walk.

Late spring, light breeze. The kind of day where the blooms have fully arrived and the air smells green and generous. I'm not rushing. I'm not chasing anything. I'm just walking, taking in what I've hiked past, what surrounds me, and what's still ahead.

This is the rhythm I trust now. Not the sprint, not the climb, but this quiet integration. Everything is here. Everything I've lived. Everything I've learned. Everything I'm still becoming.

I can see it clearly. An image of women standing together. Not performing peace, but embodying it. Not backing away from what they believe in, but standing with quiet determination, enjoying the moment and looking forward to their own *what if*.

I'm there with them.

A Reflection
There's a sweetness in looking back now. Even the sharp parts feel different through the lens of hindsight and healing. When I think about, and remember in my bones, how hard some things have been. My journey with physical pain, the ache of being an outsider, the frustration of zig-zagging toward my own definition of success... it all has a different texture now. There's more context. More compassion. And maybe even a little bit of pride.

Pressure makes diamonds. I truly believe my life would be unbearably bland without the heat and seasoning I've walked through. There are versions of me I've made peace with. I've honored the girl who kept asking, "*Am I in trouble? Am I enough?*", a question rooted in being misunderstood, in trying to stay safe, in navigating systems where I often felt unseen. I don't ask that anymore. I'm so grateful that I know I'm safe now, and I know who I am.

Living The Questions
Even after all the purposeful healing, all the purposeful growth, I still have many questions. I'm fully aware that more seasons are coming. My children will grow and leave. There may be weddings and new life and maybe someday, grandchildren. There will also be heartache. Loss. The inevitable endings that follow us all. I'm not naïve to that. I know I'll meet new chapters of pain—and I desire to learn more from those too.

But in the in-between, the questions that keep my mind reaching are often about *possibility*.

Who else will I become in this lifetime?

How else can I serve, create, influence, and inspire a better world? How else will I be humbled?

I get to continue asking my favorite question... "What if?"

This is your call to start, too. To lead, heal, disrupt, or rest. Begin wherever you are, with whatever you know. Your clarity, your rhythm, your way of being well—it's needed now.

On Legacy
The soul of this story isn't a person, rather, it's a presence. It's what rises when you stop performing and start trusting. It's the quiet strength that comes from knowing who you are, and no longer needing to prove it. This spirit lives in aligned action. In beauty with purpose.

There are things I've come to know not through studying, but through living. I know that love really does conquer all. That listening, deep, real listening, is more powerful than any pitch or platform. That presence isn't a luxury; it's the whole point. That knowing who you are and staying grounded in it will take you further than chasing applause. It's in choosing to lead, not because it's easy, but because it's yours to do.

Your legacy shows up when you decide that burnout isn't the badge you're chasing. When you remember that softness is strength. When you trust that what's meant for you isn't something you have to chase, it's something you meet when you're grounded and ready.

It lives in the woman who listens to herself. Who sets new standards time and time again, builds what she can't find, and doesn't shrink to make others comfortable. In my vision I see a ripple of grounded women creating with clarity, leading with depth, and trusting their own rhythm. Women who understand that mistakes don't disqualify you, they season you.

The soul of this book is now yours to carry forward, in the wonderfully unique way only you can.

Being Well, Now
My definition of wellness has softened, stretched, and deepened. Now, it has a gorgeous ease. It's comfort in your own skin, posture, and presence. It's the sparkle of someone grounded. It's warmth. Grace. Depth.

I find it in spaces that inspire me. In meaningful conversation. In soul-stirring art. In media that reflects truth, not noise. In people who dare to think differently, and do it kindly.

What do I hope these musings reflect? A sense of beauty. Peace. The feeling of a job done well. The kind of resonance that lingers after the meeting ends, after the retreat is over, after the consultant walks out of the room.

More than anything, I want the people in my life, Kaya, my children, my friends and family, my clients, my collaborators, to feel they were beautifully held. That their presence mattered.

Dearest Reader

Dearest reader, I remind *you*:

Your story is uniquely yours. *Who you are* is the special ingredient no one else has. If you ever find yourself doubting, undervaluing, or shrinking? Build your own table. And sit down in your full, delicious brilliance.

You are more ready than you think. More equipped. More called. More powerful. Even if it doesn't feel like it yet. Please, keep moving forward to always keep your "glass half full". What you believe is who you become. And what if you're already there?

Go live something breathtaking.

A Remembering

There's a scene, or maybe it's a dream, I keep circling back to, one from the very beginning.

Me, as a little girl, wandering through my grandparents' property. The flowers. The herbs. The berries and vegetables. I was wild and free, barefoot and blooming, held by something invisible but steady. I didn't have the words back then, but *I knew I was loved by the land and my people.*

I hold that energy close now. I stretch my ability to emulate it in the spaces I design, the work I lead, the relationships I build and keep. It was never just about the beauty. It was about how I felt in that beauty, free, supported, and well.

That's the feeling I hope this book gives you. And if not yet, then soon. I'll close my story like a storyteller calmly tucking a child into bed. The seeds have been planted. But oh, there is so much more to come.

May you rest in comfort, and rise in the sun, and live in your own authentic intention.

A Final Blessing

You are right on time
You are ready
Your gifts are needed
Now, more than ever
Lean into them now
And never hold back.

May you always...
Have a deep breath of fresh air, a peaceful home,
and a glass of your favorite drink, half full.

You deserve a life that holds you well.

Acknowledgments

No one writes a book alone. Even when the actual writing happens in quiet hours and stolen moments, the life behind it, the inspiration, the support, the strength, comes from so many others.

To Kaya, Yasira, and Atreju: My loves, thank you for being my why and my grounding force. You've each helped shape who I am, and your love lives on every page.

To my Dad, my Mom, and my stepmom Katie, thank you for loving me in your own ways and for giving me the roots to grow.

To my siblings, especially Mitch, who not only inspires me but loaned his eyes and heart as my editor. Thank you for the lifelong lessons in humor, resilience, and loyalty.

To my closest friends, especially An: thank you for holding space across the decades, asking the real questions, and always knowing when I needed a walk, a vent, or an ugly cry on a kitchen floor.

To my ancestors, my grandparents on both sides, and the long line of mothers who came before me, I carry your strength and your wounds proudly. These stories are also yours.

To my incredible team of collaborators who orbit this work. Shannon, Kate, Melissa, and others, thank you for keeping me aligned, on track, and out of my own head. Truly, I couldn't have done this without you.

To my dear pal Holly, who said, "You really should write a book, I love hearing your stories!", thank you for saying it so casually and confidently that I believed you.

To the trees, the trails, the blooms, and the quiet skies, thank you for being my co-authors. I've never felt more in flow than I did while writing this, and the land had everything to do with that.

And to you, dear reader: thank you for making space for this story. For seeing yourself in parts of it. For walking with me.

Go. Be well, and do well.

XO

Your Turn

Your Turn. Your Rhythm. Your Way.
What does it mean to you to Be Well, Do Well?

Write it. Speak it. Begin to live it.

This space is yours.

If This Book Met You at the Right Time...

There's more. You can find meditations, courses, and ways to work with me at leahcrump.com.

Whether you're returning to these pages or stepping into your next chapter, I'm so glad we found each other here.

Field Guide Index

If you're feeling...

Untethered or nostalgic → Chapter 1: Fairy Town

Craving belonging and sacred learning → Chapter 2: Initiated by Care

Ready for real, radical friendship → Chapter 3: Running With Wolves

Curious about building a life around wellness work → Chapter 4: The Business of Being Well

In the thick of healing or burnout → Chapter 5: When the Body Speaks

Reshaping your identity or boundaries → Chapter 6: The Repatterning

Stepping into sustainable leadership → Chapter 7: Arrival and Still Waters

Wanting to live your legacy now → Chapter 8: Living Well on My Own Terms

And if you ever forget what you're building... return to The Be Well, Do Well Compass.

Let it begin here.

www.ingramcontent.com/pod-product-compliance
Lightning Source LLC
Chambersburg PA
CBHW020542030426
42337CB00013B/945